Endorsements

We've known, loved, and honored Peter McHugh and his family for more than two decades now. Throughout that time, we've watched them live out their beliefs in a powerful and deeply practical way, for which we are personally grateful. It's been the joy of our lives to pursue the same ultimate goals—to receive God's grace, to be wholly transformed by it, and then to serve others so that they too might come to know their true identities as sons and daughters of God. Like Peter, we urge you never to be satisfied with intellectual knowledge of the Gospel, but to be transformed in every way as you live out the priceless inheritance you have received. This book offers many practical lessons for the journey, gathered by a kind and sincere friend—may it bless you greatly!

Heidi G. Baker, Ph.D.
Cofounder and Executive Chairman of the Board
Iris Global

Peter McHugh has been faithfully serving the Church for decades, and few lead the Body of Christ with such passion and love-driven purpose as he and his wife Lyn do. It's a privilege and a necessity that I recommend Peter's new book, *Radically Restored to Oneness with God*, as it's written with a prophetically profound perspective and gives heartfelt insight on what God desires to develop within the Church in this hour.

Whether you're a leader looking for wisdom from a trusted apostolic voice or you are a child of God who is, as Peter so perfectly phrases it, "a lifelong learner not a work-hard earner," I highly recommend you get your hands on this book and begin living in the fullness of the great grace that Christ has so abundantly afforded you.

Kris Vallotton
Leader, Bethel Church
Redding, California
Cofounder of Bethel School of Supernatural Ministry

As we endure a time in human history of tremendous division, confusion, and even accusation, we need a message and movement of unification, clarity, and honor. Again and again, I am reminded of the prayer of Jesus for us to be one with Him and with each other. The solution to today's problems is written in this equation. There is no other way to resolve this condition on the earth. This may sound desperate, but we need a global repentance. *Radically Restored to Oneness with God* is fuel for this movement. I want to highly recommend this book to all of you who want to rally right now and see Heaven saturate the earth!

Danny Silk
President and Founder of Loving on Purpose
Senior Leadership Team, Bethel Church and Jesus Culture
Redding and Sacramento, California

The title *Radically Restored to Oneness with God* is an invitation to contemplate implications inherent in the saving work of our Lord Jesus Christ. It is easy for those who have had years of Christian experience, worship, and study to assume that such things are common knowledge for believers, that there is little to be learned from such a contemplation. Although I have lived, preached, and discussed the Gospel for decades, I was repeatedly stunned, overwhelmed, and awestruck by the implications and consequences of the work of Jesus as Peter reveals it in this book. Some readers will be introduced to insights and implications they have never heard before. Some readers will be deeply challenged by observing the miracle of salvation from a perspective previously unseen. Some will be shaken as traditions and views previously perceived as truth are replaced with a salvation infinitely more gracious than tradition has ever allowed. All of us will benefit should we read slowly and deliberately. God has much to do in all of us in leading us into the experience of this radical restoration in Christ.

Dr. Allan Meyer
Cofounder, Careforce Lifekeys
Melbourne, Australia

While reading through the pages of *Radically Restored to Oneness with God*, I was captivated by the way this book quickly and continuously conveyed the heart, love, and passion of Jesus. I have had the honor of walking in covenant relationship with my friend Peter McHugh for more than a decade, and I can honestly attest that Pete truly lives what he preaches, teaches, and writes in this book. The revelation that flows through these pages is both practical and spiritual, and I was deeply moved by the Kingdom heart that beats through every word. *Radically Restored to Oneness with God* is a life-giving and life-changing book that is a must read for every Kingdom-hearted ministry leader and believer pursuing what it really means to answer the prayer of Jesus and live a life of relationship and oneness with God.

David Wagner
Founder, Father's Heart Ministries
Franklin, Tennessee

Peter McHugh's work in *Radically Restored* will put language around truths that we all know would make our world a better place. Your spirit will leap on the inside with a yes and amen. Moving Jesus from a doctrinal point on a "what we believe" pamphlet to an encounter so meaningful that it would fundamentally form the way we see our whole world is a much needed and I dare say essential exercise for followers of Christ. This book, in scripturally sound and logical fashion, helps the reader move their concept of God from existing object to insisting person. A person who holds the whole thing together and is reconciling it to Himself. This shift changes how we see our faith lived out in the world around us. My prayer is that the cry of this book would become the way the church is known in the world.

SHANE WILLARD
Shane Willard Ministries

The prayer of Jesus in John 17, "I pray also for those who will believe in me through their message, that all of them may be one, Father, just as you are in me and I am in you," is a prayer that continues to resonate generation after generation. Fathers and mothers create family, shape identity, and bring unity. Peter McHugh is one of those fathers to the Body of Christ and is carrying a powerful message that, if received, could change the way we view church and facilitate significant societal transformation.

BILLY KENNEDY
International Leader, Pioneer Network
United Kingdom

Radically Restored—the title alone stirred something inside of me when I read it. Christianity was never meant to be a tame walk but a radical journey of following Jesus. The call God has for you is radical and you will never fully be satisfied until you embrace that call. I will never forget the first time I met Peter McHugh. As we sat that week talking over meals, I was struck by the revelation that God had given him and the purity of his passion to help people move beyond the clutter and chaos of religion and experience an authentic relationship with God where true freedom is found. *Radically Restored to Oneness with God* is a message so desperately needed in this hour. This is why Jesus came—that we may know God and be restored unto Him. Peter writes with not only revelation and authority but with the heart of a father who invites us to experience the fullness of being restored to God. This book is a radical call and when embraced will change your life.

Banning Liebscher
Jesus Culture Founder and Pastor
Redding, California

Falling in love with the God whom Jesus knows can only take place as we receive, become, and release love. Peter is a great friend and more importantly a friend of God. *Radically Restored to Oneness with God* is a masterpiece that is a must read for anyone who wants to go from glory to glory. Imagine millions of believers radically restored to oneness with God resulting in the greatest harvest the world has ever seen. I say yes to this invitation! What about you?

Leif Hetland
Founder and President of Global Mission Awareness

Peter had me at the chart. I could have turned to my whiteboard immediately and begun to unpack this list of truths so dear to my heart. Our world, church, and people, are, even though they might not be aware, crying out for this. Peter is taking us on the start of a four-book journey of the world demonstrating evidence of the Kingdom of Heaven, through a church focusing on the assignment of expanding the Kingdom and individuals knowing that they are one in Him, being discipled as sons and daughters not so much to be good churchgoing Christians but ambassadors of the Kingdom. I look forward to the full set! I know from personal knowledge of Peter that this book is an expression of who he is because of the church he has built, the people who are in it, and the impact they have on their world. I expect that I will be "borrowing" his chart as I teach, always referencing the source, of course. You cannot spend time with Peter and not talk about Kingdom issues; this book will therefore be great fuel for your conversations and will adjust your narrative accordingly.

Paul Manwaring
Bethel Church Senior Leadership Team
Redding, California

It is an honor to be able to write an endorsement for Peter's new book. Endorsements are usually about the book, but I would like to endorse the author as well. *Radically Restored to Oneness with God* is not written from a leadership paradigm, though the truths contained could certainly fit into that. Rather, Peter has written this from a legacy paradigm born from a life that has been tried, tested, and trusted. He is laying stones that generations to come can build with and upon. This book, just as its title denotes, is radical, but not for the purpose of provoking a rebellion, but to provide a catalyst for reformation within the heart and life of everyone who reads it!

Gary Morgan
Cofounder, School of Prophets
Melbourne, Australia

I can't help but borrow an excerpt from Eugene Peterson's introduction to the book of Colossians (*The Message*) with respect to the quality and impact of this book: "The wedding of a brilliant and uncompromising intellect with a heart that is warmly and wonderfully kind." This is a book for today and tomorrow. God has prepared the ground for this positive biblical message to take deep root for the Kingdom of God.

Dr. Keith Farmer
Founder, Australian Christian Mentoring Network

Peter is a father in the faith to many leaders. He writes from a profound sense of surrender in the presence of God. Peter has carried for many years the heart of God for the oneness of the Body of Christ and the deep spiritual unity that God calls us to. I am honored to call Peter my friend, and all who read his work will be blessed.

DALE STEPHENSON
Senior Pastor, Crossway Church
Melbourne, Australia

My friend Peter McHugh has written a very important book for anyone who desires to be restored to wholeness. Read this book and learn from one of the best.

REV. JOSHUA MILLS
Cofounder, New Wine International
Canada

Having lived in many diverse countries, both western and eastern, I have taken note of general characteristics of these complex cultures. Western culture seems to have an inherent desire to make a system out of everything to bring greater efficiency and productivity. With the dominance of the western church over many centuries, I believe an important piece of what Jesus came to bring has been lost—oneness with Christ. Peter is calling the church back to its roots—oneness with Jesus. A passion for relationship with Christ again. It is through our relationship with Christ that we and the church are empowered, not our creative systems. This fourth book of Peter's will help many Christians to rekindle this lost culture to be *Radically Restored to Oneness with God*.

STEVE HYDE, PH.D.
Missionary to Cambodia

I felt like I was reading road signs into the future in Pete's new book, *Radically Restored to Oneness with God*. He has given us language that brings great clarity to shifts in the role of the Church God is directing all over the earth. You'll discover amazing insights how you can be more satisfied with your spiritual walk along with revelations that empower you to embrace and experience true life.

Along the way, you will no doubt connect more fully with your divine purpose. I encourage you to read *Radically Restored* thoughtfully and prayerfully as I believe through it God wants to reveal the plans, purposes, and good works He has preordained for you, the Church, and the Kingdom.

Mary Forsythe
Founder, Kingdom Living Ministries

RADICALLY RESTORED

RADICALLY RESTORED

TO ONENESS WITH GOD

*Embrace the Relationship with God
You Were Made For*

PETER McHUGH

© Copyright 2021–Peter McHugh

All rights reserved. This book is protected by the copyright laws of the United States of America. This book may not be copied or reprinted for commercial gain or profit. The use of short quotations or occasional page copying for personal or group study is permitted and encouraged. Permission will be granted upon request. Unless otherwise identified, Scripture quotations are taken from the NEW AMERICAN STANDARD BIBLE®, Copyright © 1960, 1962, 1963, 1968, 1971, 1972, 1973, 1975, 1977, 1995 by The Lockman Foundation. Used by permission. Scripture quotations marked KJV are taken from the King James Version. Scripture quotations marked MSG are taken from *The Message*. Copyright © 1993, 1994, 1995, 1996, 2000, 2001, 2002. Used by permission of NavPress Publishing Group. Scripture quotations marked AMPC are taken from the Amplified® Bible, Classic Edition, Copyright © 1954, 1958, 1962, 1964, 1965, 1987 by The Lockman Foundation. All rights reserved. Used by permission. All emphasis within Scripture quotations is the author's own. Please note that Destiny Image's publishing style capitalizes certain pronouns in Scripture that refer to the Father, Son, and Holy Spirit, and may differ from some publishers' styles. Take note that the name satan and related names are not capitalized. We choose not to acknowledge him, even to the point of violating grammatical rules.

DESTINY IMAGE® PUBLISHERS, INC.
P.O. Box 310, Shippensburg, PA 17257-0310
"Promoting Inspired Lives."

This book and all other Destiny Image and Destiny Image Fiction books are available at Christian bookstores and distributors worldwide.

Cover design by Eileen Rockwell
Interior design by Terry Clifton

For more information on foreign distributors, call 717-532-3040.
Reach us on the Internet:www.destinyimage.com.

ISBN 13 TP:978-0-7684-5782-7
ISBN 13 eBook:978-0-7684-5783-4
ISBN 13 HC:978-0-7684-5784-1
ISBN 13 LP:978-0-7684-5805-3

For Worldwide Distribution, Printed in the U.S.A.
1 2 3 4 5 6 7 8 / 25 24 23 22 21

Acknowledgments

I count it as one of the greatest privileges of my life to have served the Stairway Church community for over 30 years. From the time Lyn (my wife) and I planted the church in February 1990, our walk with God has been empowered through this wonderful congregation. They have loved us, believed in us, and carried us through some very challenging moments. The content found in the *Radically Restored* series of books has been discovered and fashioned in this context. Thank you, Stairway.

The Lord's favor on Stairway has opened the doors through which many friendships beyond Stairway have been established. These friendships have significantly impacted the way I both see my relationship with God and walk with Him. In particular, I will remain forever thankful for Bill Johnson, Graham Cooke, David Wagner, and Leif Hetland as they have released so much to me.

I write all my books by hand. That is, I pick up a pen and handwrite the first draft onto paper. My friend and personal assistant, Paula Taylor, then types my draft and subsequent handwritten edits on screen until it is ready to be sent to the publisher. Thank you, Paula, for your tireless efforts in interpreting my handwriting and your countless suggested improvements to the way I express my thoughts.

My deepest thanks go to Lyn. Our life together, the family we have raised, and the nine grandchildren we are doing our best to spoil mean more to me than words can adequately express. Lyn's love, deep conversations, shared ups and downs, and prayers are the bedrock upon which I build.

Finally and of course, the Lord—my Father God, my brother Jesus, and my instructor Holy Spirit—have made these pages possible. Thank You for trusting me with Your Word and insights. They have not just changed my life, but I have observed the profound changes in tens of thousands of people through Your encounters with them.

Contents

Foreword *by Bill Johnson* 1

Foreword *by Graham Cooke* 5

Important Note 7

Preface 11

Introduction 21

CHAPTER ONE   Our Great Salvation 31

CHAPTER TWO   The Greater Commandment 57

CHAPTER THREE   The Great Pursuit 85

CHAPTER FOUR   The Great Learning Curve 125

CHAPTER FIVE   His Great Grace 155

Conclusion 185

Foreword

I have had the great privilege of being friends with Peter McHugh for close to 15 years. I've been deeply impacted by his life as a husband and father, as well as a pastor and leader in the Body of Christ. He is one of the most genuine disciples of Jesus I've ever met. And when you add that kind of authenticity to the pastoral ministry, you usually get a <u>healthy group of Jesus-followers who really live to bring glory to God.</u> That is the case with the church he leads, Stairway Church, in Melbourne, Australia. And what they model as a church family now spills over into the lives of countless churches and leaders around the world. It is a wonder to behold.

During these years of friendship, I have had the honor of ministering to Stairway Church annually, which I always look forward to doing, in part because of the rich fellowship and time with him and his family, but also in anticipation of what they will have done with the truths I have given them the previous year. As one who travels to serve the Body of Christ at large, seeing what people do with what I have deposited is really a big deal to me. It helps me to know where the good soil is and where I should prioritize my time. And in all honesty, as I've told this body of believers on numerous occasions, I don't know of any leader or church that is more intentional in applying the insights given to them than Peter McHugh and Stairway Church. If you think about it, that's the kind of person you want to learn from. The book that you now hold in your hands was first worked out in real-life experiences, not just theories created in a classroom somewhere. From that foundation of complete devotion to Jesus, this book was written.

Radically Restored to Oneness with God is a brilliant book. It is filled—and I do mean *filled*—with insight and inspiration. And it couldn't come at a better time. With much of the world in chaos and the church often mirroring the instability of our surroundings, *Radically Restored* is given that we might become established in truth and from there reveal the absolute rock, Christ Jesus. Nothing can move such a rock. Our fears, wrong teachings, and self-absorption all create an atmosphere of instability that is opposite to the nature of Christ, and thus the nature of our salvation. This book was written to help correct that problem while creating the joyful expectation that comes from Christ alone.

The truth will set you free. This statement has been quoted often by various parts of society, sometimes ungodly in nature, to add credibility to their opinion about various subjects. But it was Jesus who made this statement. He is the Way, the Truth, and the Life. So then, real truth is a person. And when He sets people free, it's always *unto* something. In other words, in Christ we are set free *from* something, *unto* something. If you imagine a prisoner being released from prison back into society, but they are homeless and jobless, you can picture the weakness of our understanding of freedom. They have experienced freedom *from*, but tragically not *unto*. That ex-prisoner is free, but not completely. In Christ, it is different. We are freed from sin. But it doesn't end there. In Christ we are freed unto His nature, and into His entire personal inheritance from the Father. *Radially Restored* is all about the *unto*.

You're about to enter a journey where you will discover who Jesus says we are, that we might fully enter the life He purchased for us at the cross and made possible through His resurrection. This journey is what we were born for. Welcome to the adventure of a lifetime.

BILL JOHNSON
Bethel Church
Redding, California
Author of *Born for Significance* and *The Way of Life*

Foreword

Any message that has an anti-church stance is not representing the Kingdom. Jesus came to model the Kingdom, to showcase the Nature of His Father, and to create the means of salvation to be received as a gift.

In doing so, He gave us permission to become bilocational—to live on earth as we would in Heaven. Full salvation is the majesty of God inside the smallness of man. We are receiving His presence, not as increments of blessing but as an ever-increasing reality of His passion for us.

Our lives are marked by the Fruit of the Spirit in the constant development of God's nature living in us. Fullness is not an option. It is our only choice! We simply cannot ever allow a theology that empowers the enemy and limits humanity.

The purpose and the process of Christ in us is what elevates our identity to a level that delights God's sovereignty.

God loves life on our level and is inviting us to live on His! The first definitive statement that He made about mankind preceded our introduction to the world: "Let Us make man in Our image, according to Our likeness" (Gen. 1:26). This is known as primary purpose. He has been faithful to that purpose for thousands of years and with countless millions of people.

It is the neglect of that purpose that has caused His Body to occupy a lesser place in the world. We have become a refuge from change rather than the engine room of transformation. The state of the world is the evidence of our lack in the Kingdom.

I have been privileged to know Peter McHugh—the man, the thinker, and the leader. I know his passion to be the fullest expression of Christ possible both as an individual and as part of the corporate man in Christ.

For twenty years, as a visiting ministry, we have spent considerable time in conversation, question, and dialogue—our own personal think tank that has changed us both. I have thoroughly enjoyed time with family, playing cricket in the yard with grandkids, and lively conversation with much life, love, and laughter in the family.

This book is an extension of Peter and Lyn's heart and passion for an authentic lifestyle that resonates with the beating heart of Jesus. It is both true and truth, filled with grace and the beauty of God's character and nature. You will find more than principles, values, and practices. You will discover a presence that will call you up to a higher level of relationship and a deeper understanding of true fellowship.

Your own heart will be strangely warmed. Your calling in leadership, gift, and ministry will be generated by a higher focus and a deeper, more urgent need to serve God to the fullest.

We cannot go back to our forefathers in the early church; we must go forward to become the generation that prepares the Bride. We need to become the generation that prepares the Bride. We need to become the friends of the Bridegroom who will empower His Beloved to take back all that has been robbed from her.

When the Bride is at the height, beauty, and majesty, only then will the King come for His Beloved.

Graham Cooke
BrilliantTV.com

Important Note

...to be read carefully

WHY DO I QUOTE AND RE-PRESENT, IN FULL, SO MUCH OF THE WORD in what I have written?

There are two reasons.

The first is that the Barna Research Group, regarding religion in 2009, made the following observations:

> Most self-identified Christians are comfortable with the idea that the Bible and the sacred books from non-Christian religions all teach the same truths and principles.
>
> ...Bible reading has become the religious equivalent of sound-bite journalism. When people read from the Bible they typically open it, read a brief passage without much regard for the context, and consider the primary thought or feeling that the passage provided. If they are comfortable with it, they accept it; otherwise, then deem it interesting but irrelevant to their life, and move on. There is shockingly little growth evident in people's understanding of the fundamental themes of the scriptures and amazingly little interest in deepening their knowledge and application of biblical principles.[1]

The second is that in Mark 4:1-12, Matthew 13:1-15, and Luke 8:4-10 Jesus told the parable of the sower and the seed. The disciples were unable to understand what they were hearing and asked for an explanation. Jesus began His explanation by telling His disciples that in this parable, they had been given *the* mystery or key to the Kingdom of God.

The mystery or key is that all spiritual truth and subsequent insight and revelation comes in the form of a seed, and that seed is the Word of God.

As I came to write these four books, I was aware of the Holy Spirit imploring me to, as much as possible, not just give reference to the Word of God but to actually quote it for all to read. I am convinced that our journey of discipleship, transformation, and spiritual maturity is enhanced, empowered, and accelerated when the Spirit and Word come together in a moment of insight that takes root in our heart and grows through application.

Without the seed of God's Word, our spiritual lives wither away, and our capacity to represent Jesus well is limited. Deuteronomy 8:3 declares an eternal perspective of our need for the Word:

> *He humbled you and let you be hungry, and fed you with manna which you did not know, nor did your fathers know, that He might make you understand that man does not live by bread alone, but man lives by everything that proceeds out of the mouth of the Lord.*

Equally, the other essential ingredient to the seed, the Word, is the soil or heart posture and condition of the one reading and receiving the Word. The seed carries the same potential to change a life and the world around them to everyone who hears. Yet that potential is only released fully through those who have humble and meek hearts who want to fully surrender to the Lordship of Jesus. Jesus, when speaking to those who had believed Him yet were seeking to kill Him, observed in John 8:37 that this was the case: *"because My word has no entrance (makes no progress, does not find any place) in you"* (AMPC).

My strongest encouragement to you as you come to this material is to purposefully read the quoted Word of God through a prayerfully surrendered heart that longs to do what you know to do in receiving, becoming, and releasing the love of God.

Note

1. Barna Group, "Barna Studies the Research, Offers a Year-in-Review Perspective," December 20, 2009, https://www.barna.com/research/barna-studies-the-research-offers-a-year-in-review-perspective.

Preface

Have you ever driven in Italy?

I have, and it is quite an experience after driving in Australia for 45 years.

The overarching philosophy of drivers in Italy is an aggressive mind-set of everyone for themselves where you don't give an inch. This translates into the following practices:

- Hesitation means you are not going;
- The left lane is *only* for passing at high speeds;
- Stop signs mean "make sure the coast is clear before proceeding," *not* "stop";
- Horns are a mode of communication, *not* anger;
- Drive aggressively to fit into gaps and do not care for what is going on behind you; and
- Use blinkers when changing lanes to say "here I go" *not* "I want to go" or "I'm waiting to see if you will let me go."

When I first started driving in Italy, I was completely unaware of these practices. However, after the first week, I became familiar with this new mind-set; it started to make sense, and I strangely appreciated it!

Across the Body of Christ, there is a rising prophetic voice calling God's people to become familiar with the practices required to be an answer to Jesus' prayer.

> *I do not ask on behalf of these alone, but for those also who believe in Me through their word; that they may all be one; even as You, Father, are in Me and I in You, that they also may be in Us, so that the world may believe that You sent Me. The glory which You have given Me I have given to them, that they may be one, just as We are one; I in them and You in Me, that they may be perfected in unity, so that the world may know that You sent Me, and loved them, even as You have loved Me* (John 17:20-23).

Greg Boyd, in his book *Repenting of Religion*, writes:

> We must confess that Jesus' prayer for the church to manifest the perfect, loving unity of the triune God has by and large not been fulfilled. Whatever else the church may be known for in the world, it is not generally known for exemplifying a distinctive, radical, self-sacrificial love, either toward those within the body of Christ or toward those without. The church generally has not left people with the impression that we are unique in the way we affirm the unsurpassable worth of each individual regardless of how immoral and unlovable he or she may be.
>
> If anything, the church today is largely known for its petty divisiveness along denominational, doctrinal, social, and even racial lines. On the whole, it is perceived as being *less* loving and *less* accepting than most other communities. It is often known for its self-proclaimed and often hypocritical alliance with good against evil and for its

judgmentalism toward those it concludes are *evil*. But, tragically, as a corporate body it rarely is known as being distinctive because of its radical love. In contrast to Jesus' prayer, the world is *not* compelled to believe in the triune God on the grounds that his love is undeniably present among Jesus' disciples.[1]

Similarly, Andy Stanley, in his book *Irresistible*, writes:

…Imagine a world where people were skeptical of what we believed but envious of how well we treated one another…Once upon a time it was so. Once upon a time the *one-another* culture of the church stood in sharp contrast to the "bite and devour" one-another culture of the pagan world.… Paul's *one-another* list should epitomize the reputation of those who call themselves Christians. When people outside the church think about folks inside the church, the items on Paul's list should come to mind.… After all, Paul said, "the only thing that counts is faith expressing itself through love."[2]

As well as joining myself to this growing chorus of voices, I'm writing this series of books, *Radically Restored*, in response to the Lord's call on my life. This became dramatically clear to me in March 2018 when my wife Lyn and I travelled from Melbourne, Australia to Adelaide, Australia for a weekend of ministry.

I have had the privilege of travelling a great deal over the last 25 years. When we arrived in Adelaide, we went to collect our bag from the carousel and found our bag was the first to come off the plane. This had never happened before, nor has it happened since to date. At the time, I felt prompted to take note.

We were then taken to our accommodation for the time we were staying in Adelaide. There were six units on a beach setting, and we were in Apartment One. I was again prompted to take note and was intrigued by how the Lord may be attempting to show me something through the number "one."

Over the next few hours, I became convinced that when we went to dinner that night, we would be seated at table number one. I spoke to Lyn about what I was observing and sensing, including being seated at table number one. We went for dinner with our hosts who knew nothing of what was taking place, and we were all shown to table number one.

The Lord then proceeded to show off and make His point abundantly clear. When we returned to Melbourne, we were waiting at carousel number two for our bag with all the other passengers. Another passenger had collected their bag, and as the available area is very small, they were moving behind me to leave the building. I turned to make sure they had enough room to get past. As I turned, I saw one bag on carousel number one, with no passengers waiting there, and it was my bag!

In the preceding months leading to this ministry trip to Adelaide, I had been on a journey with the Lord in my devotional life. I was hearing Him unpack thoughts about reconciled diversity being a key to how God's people could be an answer to Jesus' prayer in John 17:20-23. All of these events during this ministry trip strongly affirmed that He was asking me to carry this message of oneness—that is, reconciled diversity—wherever I could. This four-book series *Radically Restored* has come to life.

The term *reconciled diversity* means that we reconcile within ourselves that expressions of the Kingdom of God through the many denominations, movements, and networks are not to be seen as requiring change or adjustment. We all need relationships for *identity*. There were twelve tribes in the nation of Israel, each with their particular role to play and land to occupy. They were not focused on trying to change the other tribes, asserting that their tribe was right and the others wrong, nor making it clear that their tribe was better than the others. They acknowledged diversity as being what it was.

For followers of Jesus to be an answer to Jesus' prayer of being one requires a heart posture of being reconciled to the fact that we will not agree on everything. While we agree on ninety-five percent of theological questions, we are called to agree to disagree about the remaining five percent. We need to avoid striving to prove who is right and who is wrong. Equally, the ways we practice our faith are diverse, and we are called to honor and respect the traditions and ways of prayer and worship found across the Body of Christ. As we adopt the perspective of reconciled diversity, we begin to look to relationship for *impact*. Jesus declared our oneness would result in the world knowing the Father had sent the Son.

When we put our trust in Jesus, when we are born again, we are radically restored into oneness with God (see John 17:21). Jesus promised that when we placed our faith in Him through repentance that the Godhead would make their abode in us. We would no longer be orphans (see John 14:18). Paul understands this to be a mystery: *"which is Christ in you, the hope of glory"* (Col. 1:27). Paul describes this radical restoration as *"receiving the adoption as sons"* (Gal. 4:5).

Understandably, the profound nature of this restoration has significant implications for how disciples who want to reveal Jesus live out their personal spirituality and journey (see Rom. 8:29; 1 John 4:15-17). To help us understand this significance, Jesus rewrote the second of the two great commandments of the Old Testament. He moved from "love one another as you love yourself," to "love one another, *as I have loved you*." In so doing, He expects us (it is a command) to know in our hearts, through experience and encounter, the love God has for us. This surpasses the more familiar experiences for us of knowing something intellectually (see Eph. 3:19). This knowledge was so profoundly significant to Paul in establishing the church that he wrote:

> *But the goal of our instruction is love from a pure heart and a good conscience and a sincere faith* (1 Timothy 1:5).

Jesus makes it clear that the radical restoration of being one with God needs to flow into a radical restoration of being one with one another. The outcome of these radical restorations is societal transformation. That is, *"the world may believe that You sent Me"* (John 17:20-21)

The apostle Peter recognized the significance of understanding that being radically restored to oneness with God should result in our pursuit of being radically restored to oneness with one another. In Second Peter 1:5, he writes, *"Now for this very reason also, applying…."* In verses two to four, Peter describes how we have become one with God and can now live in oneness with God by "becoming partakers of the divine nature." It is for this reason that we are to apply ourselves to a lifestyle that ultimately results in brotherly kindness and love—that is, oneness with others.

Peter then stresses the absolute centrality of building our spirituality on oneness with God and one another when he declares:

> *For if these qualities are yours and are increasing, they render you neither useless nor unfruitful in the true knowledge of our Lord Jesus Christ. For he who lacks these qualities is blind or short-sighted, having forgotten his purification from his former sins* (2 Peter 1:8-9).

It then appears that he is not content that he has adequately explained the significance of following Jesus through a focus on oneness with God and others, and so he then goes on to write:

Therefore, brethren, be all the more diligent to make certain about His calling and choosing you; for as long as you practice these things, you will never stumble; for in this way the entrance into the eternal kingdom of our Lord and Savior Jesus Christ will be abundantly supplied to you (2 Peter 1:10-11).

Why does any Church exist?

Church as an end in itself		Church as a means to the coming of the Kingdom
to growth	KEYS	to Kingdom
based in achievement	VALUES	based in Who we reveal
of the church	DISCIPLES	who learn to walk with God
servant	IDENTITY	son/daughter
develop & manage programs	LEADERS	empower spiritual growth
gifts/skills/ability/practices/ activity-led	LEADERS FOCUS	personal spirituality life/presence/oneness
functional relationships to grow church numbers	WINESKIN	personal relationships that grow people who advance the Kingdom
telling for the purpose of agreement	COMMUNICATION STYLE	understanding for the purpose of knowing and being known
provision functional (tasks) circumstantial role & position principles (outcomes) shoulder to shoulder	SPIRITUAL FOCUS	promises relational (honor) spiritual struggles & triumphs presence (heart transformation) heart to heart
seating capacity	SUNDAY	sending capacity (assignments)
earth to heaven unity of purpose	PRAYER	heaven to earth unity of heart

Finally, he sees it as a privilege and necessity to definitely remind them of the need to live this way from oneness with God and others. Even when he has passed away, they would call this teaching to mind.

> *Therefore, I will always be ready to remind you of these things, even though you already know them, and have been established in the truth which is present with you. I consider it right, as long as I am in this earthly dwelling, to stir you up by way of reminder, knowing that the laying aside of my earthly dwelling is imminent, as also our Lord Jesus Christ has made clear to me. And I will also be diligent that at any time after my departure you will be able to call these things to mind* (2 Peter 1:12-15).

Today, like Greg Boyd and Andy Stanley, I hear the Spirit asking me as a church leader to reexamine how at Stairway—the church that Lyn and I planted in 1990 and still lead—we live together as God's people. With the governance teams of Stairway, we have identified the need to become a different sort of "driver" of the vehicle called the church. To no longer drive with the practices associated with church being an end in itself but rather to learn to drive with the practices associated with the church being a means to the coming of the Kingdom.

Jesus came *"proclaiming the gospel of the Kingdom"* (Matt. 4:23). He taught us to pray, *"Your Kingdom come"* (Matt. 6:10). Jesus called us to *"seek first His Kingdom"* (Matt. 6:33). Countless theologians have approached finding the Kingdom of God in many different ways. For me, the most concise definition is: "Where the supreme rule and reign of Jesus exists." The activity of those who proclaim, pray for, and seek first the Kingdom is "to restore everything back to the way God originally intended things to be." God's original intent for all mankind was that they live in oneness with God and oneness with one another. That mankind would bear witness to the covenant community of love that characterizes the Trinity.

Preface

The four-book series *Radically Restored* is written to help the reader on their journey of being a disciple who reveals Jesus and bears witness to the Kingdom of God in the way they live their lives.

- Book One: *Radically Restored to Oneness with God*
- Book Two: *Radically Restored to Oneness with One Another*
- Book Three: *Radically Restored to Release Oneness for Societal Transformation*
- Book Four: *Radically Restored Leadership Practices for Establishing a Culture of Oneness*

I welcome you to a journey based on curiosity and discovery with a view to a reformation for God's people and His Church.

Notes

1. Greg Boyd, *Repenting of Religion: Turning from Judgment to the Love of God* (Grand Rapids, MI: Baker Books, 2004), 46.
2. Andy Stanley, *Irresistible: Reclaiming the New That Jesus Unleashed for the World* (Grand Rapids, MI: Zondervan, 2020), 216-217.

Introduction

Who am I?

This was the painful and confusing pursuit of my adolescent years that I carried into my twenties. I wonder whether it was for you…or maybe it still is!

Philosophers wrestle with this question. In answer to the question, "Who am I," the philosopher René Descartes made popular the well-known dictum: *I think, therefore I am.* A more complex synthesis from the thoughts of philosophers is that *I am directly to me, the given integrity of my individual.* I perceive myself as the center of my consciousness, as someone who owns my thoughts, desires, and experiences. At the same time, I am the unity of my biography; this is what guarantees my self-identity. Finally, I am what controls my body; it is the instance that answers the free adoption of my decisions and is responsible for their implementation and consequences.

My adolescent self did not ponder these complexities. For me, it was a little more concrete and precise. For example, who am I as a son, brother, student, friend, and water polo player? What do others think of me in these roles, and how are their expectations going to shape me? What will I do to be a successful adult, and is that who I am destined to be? How do I prove myself, and on what basis? Who do I assert my opinions and points of view to, at least be heard and at best to be right?

The other intangible question that my adolescent self confronted was, *Why am I here?* Oh, the pain of not being sure!

Both the "*Who am I?*" and "*Why am I here?*" questions originate from the space in all of our hearts that wants to belong, be significant, and be secure. We have been created with these three primary motivations. Having travelled to over 30 countries in the world and having studied human history—having had the joy of doing life with thousands of people from many, many cultures—it is absolutely clear to me that we are all the same in this respect.

If you examine your own inner world, your feelings, and self-talk, I am convinced you will find that your responses and reactions all find their motivation to satisfy the need to belong, to be significant, and to be secure. This is the desire to fit somewhere with a group of like-minded people. It is the heartache for community that we all pursue.

Intrinsically, we are all searching for an identity. Who am I? Why am I here? In the 21st century, this pursuit is clearly seen in the use of social media. The way people project their lives and lifestyles along with their opinions and views. The apparent success of reality TV is our fascination with the way others are trying to find themselves in a variety of communal settings. The cult of celebrity plays into the place of comparing my life to something that I would aspire to, that I would want to be. The acceptance of what the fashion industry decides is the current way we need to present ourselves to belong to the most up-to-date crowd. All our searching and longing to know—who am I and why am I here? What is my identity?

Kinnaman and Matlock sharpen the significance and importance of this topic when making disciples aged between 18 and 29.

> The battle to define identity is one reason disciple making is so difficult today…In digital Babylon our screens grant us access to a plethora of identity-forming tools, communities and adventures…Algorithms that run apps

provide helpful suggestions for our identity-forming efforts...What we consume stakes a claim on who we are and that is the stuff of identity...Ironically, however, most of us end up looking like the crowd we want to be a part of; the apparent value placed on self-expression is actually driven by someone else's preferences. Even when we think we're marching to our own beat, we've got an unseen drummer in our heads, keeping time and making claims on our identity...most people today, including Christians, believe identity can be discovered and decided by the individual...Contrary to the Creator's intentions, human identity is under a full-scale rebrand in digital Babylon. Personal screens reinforce the notion of elective identity by giving us daily, even hourly, chances to present a self-selected, carefully filtered, curated version of ourselves to friends and followers. Social media, for all its promises to connect people, also feeds our worst individualist, brand-making impulses by asking us to present (or perform) our "personal brand guidelines" on Facebook, Twitter, and Instagram. Every day the message is reinforced: you get to—you must—define who you are...But we must persuade young exiles that the truest thing about humans is what our Creator says about us: that we are created with essential worth and dignity as children crafted in his image that following his Son, Jesus, restores his image in us, which was broken as a result of human rebellion.[1]

Jesus, the wisest and most insightful person who has ever lived, addresses these matters when He meets Zaccheus as recorded in Luke 19:1-10:

> *He entered Jericho and was passing through. And there was a man called by the name of Zaccheus; he was a chief tax collector and he was rich. Zaccheus was trying to see who Jesus was, and was unable because of the crowd, for he was small in stature. So he ran on ahead and climbed up into a sycamore tree in order to see Him, for He was about to pass through that way. When Jesus came to the place, He looked up and said to him, "Zaccheus, hurry and come down, for today I must stay at your house." And he hurried and came down and received Him gladly. When they saw it, they all began to grumble, saying, "He has gone to be the guest of a man who is a sinner." Zaccheus stopped and said to the Lord, "Behold, Lord, half of my possessions I will give to the poor, and if I have defrauded anyone of anything, I will give back four times as much." And Jesus said to him, "Today salvation has come to this house, because he, too, is a son of Abraham. For the Son of Man has come to seek and to save that which was lost."*

As Luke tells us this true story, he introduces four descriptions about who Zaccheus is. The first thing we are told about Zaccheus is that he is "a chief tax collector." How often do we and others find part of our identity in what we do? I travel and meet many people on planes. More often than not, one of the early questions in a conversation when meeting others for the first time is "What do you do?" As well as being genuinely interested, what is really happening is that we are figuring out "How am I to relate to you?" (Interestingly, this also affects how we relate to ourselves.)

When I am asked what I do, I have found entirely different responses to me depending on how I self-identify. If I say I am a pastor, the conversation at best becomes awkward and at worst abruptly ceases! Those I tell clearly have preconceived ideas about Christians and "men of the cloth." If I say I am an international speaker and author (which I am!), then the conversation becomes very animated from others as they are intrigued to know more.

Similarly, in the year after I finished school and went to university, I worked as an orderly at a hospital. Hospitals are very hierarchical in their work relationships. Brain surgeons are highly respected and honored. However, in my day, cleaners and orderlies were the least respected and honored people. The hospital staff made assumptions about who I was based on my role. They didn't take the time to know me, my history, or my dreams for the future.

Steve Waugh, a great captain and player in the Australian cricket team from 1985 to 2004, in his autobiography wrote some honest and vulnerable comments about himself, including:

> Like others, I often equated my overall worth with my performances on the field. Foolhardily, I believed I was a lesser person if I failed and more worthy if I did well. For the five weeks from my selection in the first Test to my hundred in Sydney, the cricket headlines seemed to dominate, and my field of vision narrowed to a point where all I could see was my name and personality being dissected piece by piece. Gradually I became more agitated, and the jaundiced views I formed began to eat away at every aspect of my life.[2]

These examples and your life experience demonstrate that culture powerfully answers the questions of "Who am I and why am I here?" based on what we do. Zaccheus, as a tax collector, was shunned by his own people, the Jews. As a Jew, he collected money for the Roman oppressors of his people and occupiers of their land. He used his position corruptly to take more than was due to line his own pockets. He was despised by his own people and at best pitied by the Romans.

Personally, my identity—that is, my sense of value, my understanding of my self-worth, my well-being, and my security—is not influenced by what I do. Who I am and why I am here are not defined by the culture I live in or the role I play in that culture. What about for you?

The second thing we are told about Zaccheus is that he is rich. James identifies that culture again ascribes value and worth and matters of identity based on wealth.

> *For if a man comes into your assembly with a gold ring and dressed in fine clothes, and there also comes in a poor man in dirty clothes, and you pay special attention to the one who is wearing the fine clothes, and say, "You sit here in a good place," and you say to the poor man, "You stand over there, or sit down by my footstool," have you not made distinctions among yourselves, and become judges with evil motives?*
> (James 2:2-4)

We are all unconsciously educated to know ourselves and others, in part, based on material wealth. We identify things about ourselves and others based on the cars people drive, the suburbs in which they live, the size of their houses, the clothes and jewelry worn, and so on. Is this you?

The third thing we are told about Zaccheus is that he is small in stature. I'm not the greatest fan of shopping. However, when I do go to shopping malls, I can't help but notice how dominated they are by consumer opportunities to buy stuff for the dressing up of our appearance. The point of entry for most department stores is flooded with the chance to purchase cosmetics followed by clothing for both men and women.

Different sectors of society identify as a group through the same clothes, hairstyles, tattoos, etc. If you are a gang member, you dress accordingly. Male executives tend to come to business meetings in suits, and male politicians attend parliament in suits. Others identify with sporting heroes by wearing team colors with the hero's number and name on them.

Everyone is aware of the gender imbalance in the workforce for high-paying corporate roles. Political parties have quotas for female representation. Ethnic and religious prejudice affects employment opportunities so that all these aspects of what we look like affect how we see ourselves and where we fit.

I am not for a minute being critical of these phenomena. I am hoping to offer commentary that helps us to ponder and consider the influences that inform our well-being, value, and worth—our source of identity. That is, how we answer the questions "Who am I and why am I here?"

The fourth thing we are told about Zaccheus is that he is "a sinner." That is, his identity is evaluated based on his spiritual worth, the value of his character, and how "well" he has performed. In our prevalent pursuit to belong, to be significant, and to be secure, we endeavor to meet these needs by answering the question, "What is right and required for acceptance?" Invariably, we find answers based on performance. That is performance deemed to be appropriate by the significant social groups in our lives. These behaviors can have spiritual overlay. However, they all have a cultural overlay.

Consequently, we find ourselves in what others expect of us. We define ourselves through the values of others. That is how I see myself—who I am is a reflection of how others see me. My value and worth are ascribed to me based on conditions that evaluate my performance.

We all have similar influences that shape our answers to the big questions of life—who am I and why am I here. Our values, worth, and well-being are shaped and formed by the influence of what we do, what we have, what we look like, and how we perform. Our identity invariably is an amalgam of these influences. This leaves us vulnerable to the power of fear and living with self-talk that is self-condemning, self-centered attitudes, and a self-reliant lifestyle.

We live with the fear that we won't measure up to the expectations of others and ourselves. We live with the fear that if people really knew who we are, they wouldn't like us. We live with the fear that our lives aren't as meaningful or valuable as others.

Fear always results in the need for a fight or flight. Therefore, we do what is best for us (self-centered). We live life in our strength (self-reliant), invariably making mistakes while feeling isolated and living with accumulated failure (self-condemning).

It is at this point that Jesus enters Zaccheus' story. It is in these conundrums that Jesus' presence elevates Zaccheus to a new way of being. It is in this environment Jesus speaks into the turmoil of Zaccheus' pursuit for identity and answers to "Who am I and why am I here?"

Summary

- Intrinsically, we are all searching for an identity: "Who am I?"
- That search is often explored and answered through:
  - What I do
  - What I have (wealth and material assets)
  - How I view my physical appearance
  - My assessment of my character and performance
- The amalgam of these answers leaves us vulnerable to fear, which creates self-talk that is self-condemning, attitudes that are self-centered, and lifestyles that are self-reliant.

Questions and Activities

1. Write a paragraph that describes how you know and see yourself.
2. Write a paragraph that describes how you think others know and see you.
3. What are you afraid of, and does it impact the way you respond to yourself, to others, and to the circumstances of life?

Note

1. David Kinnaman and Mark Matlock, *Faith for Exiles* (Grand Rapids, MI: Baker Books, 2019), 45-48.
2. Steve Waugh, *Out of My Comfort Zone: The Autobiography* (Penguin Group Australia, 2015).

Chapter One

OUR GREAT SALVATION

Jesus came to save something…
that is at the core of everyone.

THERE IS A STORY THAT HAS BEEN SHARED OFTEN IN RECENT YEARS:

Years ago, before transatlantic flight was common, a man wanted to travel to the United States from Europe. The man worked hard, saved every extra penny he could, and finally had just enough money to purchase a ticket aboard a cruise ship. The trip at that time required about two or three weeks to cross the ocean. He went out and bought a suitcase and filled it full of cheese and crackers. That's all he could afford. Once on board, all the other passengers went to the large, ornate dining room to eat their gourmet meals. Meanwhile, the poor man would go over in the corner and eat his cheese and crackers. This went on day after day. He could smell the delicious food being served in the dining room. He heard the other passengers speak of it in glowing terms as they rubbed their bellies and complained about how full they were, and how they would have to go on a diet after this trip. The poor traveler wanted to join the other guests in the dining room, but he had no extra money. Sometimes he'd lie awake at night dreaming of the sumptuous meals the other guests described. Toward the end of the trip, another man came up to him and said, "Sir, I can't help but notice that you are always over there eating those cheese and crackers at mealtimes. Why don't you come to the banquet hall and eat with us?" The traveler's face flushed with embarrassment. "Well to tell you the truth, I had only enough money to buy the ticket. I don't have any extra money to purchase fancy meals." The other passenger raised his eyebrows in surprise. He shook his head and said, "Sir, don't you realize the meals are included in the price of the ticket? Your meals have already been paid for!"[1]

There are times when we miss out on all the Lord has won for us due to a lack of knowledge. Luke 19:9-10, the conclusion of the story of Zacchaeus eating with Jesus, states:

> *And Jesus said to him, "Today salvation has come to this house, because he, too, is a son of Abraham. For the Son of Man has come to seek and to save that which was lost."*

Jesus declared of Himself here in verse 10 that he came to seek and save "that which was lost." The original language is not "those who are lost." However, that is how paraphrased, modern versions of the Scripture often interpret the original language.

When Jesus announced that salvation had come to Zaccheus' house, he said it was *"because he, too, is a son of Abraham."* Jesus indicated that Zaccheus' salvation restored his *identity* as a son of Abraham. So the "that" or "what" which was lost that Jesus came to save was our identity. Jesus hadn't died and risen from the dead yet. The only identity that was available for Zacchaeus to be restored to was that of "a son of Abraham." However, Galatians 4:4-7 promises our restored identity as sons/children of God:

> *But when the fullness of the time came, God sent forth His Son, born of a woman, born under the Law, so that He might redeem those who were under the Law, that we might receive the adoption as sons. Because you are sons, God has sent forth the Spirit of His Son into our hearts, crying, "Abba! Father!" Therefore you are no longer a slave, but a son; and if a son, then an heir through God.*

When you put your trust in Jesus, when you were born again, and when you were saved, Jesus fulfilled the Father's intent that He stated in John 14:23:

> *Jesus answered and said to him, "If anyone loves Me, he will keep My word; and My Father will love him, and We will come to him and make Our abode with him."*

Just before this promise, Jesus declared in John 14:16-18:

> *I will ask the Father, and He will give you another Helper, that He may be with you forever; that is the Spirit of truth, whom the world cannot receive, because it does not see Him or know Him, but you know Him because He abides with you and will be in you. I will not leave you as orphans; I will come to you.*

This is why Jesus prays in John 17:20-21:

> *I do not ask on behalf of these alone, but for those also who believe in Me through their word; that they may all be one; even as You, Father, are in Me and I in You, that they also may be in Us, so that the world may believe that You sent Me.*

Paul understood this mystery when he wrote:

to whom God willed to make known what is the riches of the glory of this mystery among the Gentiles, which is Christ in you, the hope of glory (Colossians 1:27).

Paul recognized the importance of understanding this truth when he wrote:

Test yourselves to see if you are in the faith; examine yourselves! Or do you not recognize this about yourselves, that Jesus Christ is in you—unless indeed you fail the test? (2 Corinthians 13:5)

This is why Paul describes that our reality as followers of Jesus is:

for in Him we live and move and exist, as even some of your own poets have said, "For we also are His children" (Acts 17:28).

Equally, John affirms that our role in the world is to be like Jesus in our daily lives:

Whoever confesses that Jesus is the Son of God, God abides in him, and he in God. We have come to know and have believed the love which God has for us. <u>God is love, and the one who abides in love abides in God, and God</u> abides in him. By this, love is perfected with us, so that we may have confidence in the day of judgment; because as He is, so also are we in this world (1 John 4:15-17).

Without the revelation of these truths, we do not live lives that give Jesus His full reward. We do not realize the extraordinary inheritance we have been given through our restored oneness with God and a new identity as children of God:

giving thanks to the Father, who has qualified us to share in the inheritance of the saints in Light (Colossians 1:12).

Nor do we pursue Him in the transformation to fulfill our destiny to be like Him in every way.

> *For those whom He foreknew, He also predestined to become conformed to the image of His Son, so that He would be the firstborn among many brethren* (Romans 8:29).

So the whole earth is groaning that we live fully in our new identity, our restored oneness with God, so that His Kingdom would come and His will be done for the benefit of your family, friends, neighbors, work colleagues, and those we study with.

> *Therefore from now on we recognize no one according to the flesh; even though we have known Christ according to the flesh, yet now we know Him in this way no longer. Therefore if anyone is in Christ, he is a new creature; the old things passed away; behold, new things have come. Now all these things are from God, who reconciled us to Himself through Christ and gave us the ministry of reconciliation, namely, that God was in Christ reconciling the world to Himself, not counting their trespasses against them, and He has committed to us the word of reconciliation. Therefore, we are ambassadors for Christ, as though God were making an appeal through us; we beg you on behalf of Christ, be reconciled to God. He made Him who knew no sin to be sin on our behalf, so that we might become the righteousness of God in Him* (2 Corinthians 5:16-21).

In His unbounded love, God became what we are (human) so that we might become what He is. Christ in us means we can live in the same realm as Jesus.

> *Therefore if you have been raised up with Christ, keep seeking the things above, where Christ is, seated at the right hand*

of God. Set your mind on the things above, not on the things that are on earth. For you have died and your life is hidden with Christ in God (Colossians 3:1-3).

We are to learn through a relational process of transformation to live and walk with God from a place of abiding in Him.

I am the vine, you are the branches; he who abides in Me and I in him, he bears much fruit, for apart from Me you can do nothing (John 15:5).

If you abide in Me, and My words abide in you, ask whatever you wish, and it will be done for you (John 15:7).

Just as the Father has loved Me, I have also loved you; abide in My love. If you keep My commandments, you will abide in My love; just as I have kept My Father's commandments and abide in His love (John 15:9-10).

God wants to walk with us in and through the complete confidence that we are accepted by Him as we are:

Blessed be the God and Father of our Lord Jesus Christ, who has blessed us with every spiritual blessing in the heavenly places in Christ, just as He chose us in Him before the foundation of the world, that we would be holy and blameless before Him. In love He predestined us to adoption as sons through Jesus Christ to Himself, according to the kind intention of His will, to the praise of the glory of His grace, which He freely bestowed on us in the Beloved. In Him we have redemption through His blood, the forgiveness of our trespasses, according to the riches of His grace which He lavished on us. In all wisdom and insight He made known to us the mystery of His will, according to His kind intention which He purposed in Him (Ephesians 1:3-9).

Oneness Lost and the Consequences

Luke 19:9-10 makes it clear that Jesus came to seek and save something that was lost—that is, a *that* or *what* which is a part of those who put their faith in Him. Jesus came to seek and to save something at the core of everyone—our identity—because whoever believes in Him receives eternal life and begins living with God as His child.

What other evidence is there that our identity was lost?

Great question.

Genesis 3:1-12 holds the key.

Adam and Eve had been created by God. God walked with them as their Father. They were living in the Garden in oneness with God, deeply loved by Him and accepted as His children. Satan then came into the Garden to tempt Adam and Eve to do what their Father had asked them not to do.

The temptation was designed so that they would exchange their oneness with God for being like God in knowing good from evil.

> *The serpent said to the woman, "You surely will not die! For God knows that in the day you eat from it your eyes will be opened, and you will be like God, knowing good and evil"* (Genesis 3:4-5).

When Adam and Eve believed the temptation and ate of the fruit, they exchanged one father for another on behalf of all mankind.

> *You are of your father the devil, and you want to do the desires of your father. He was a murderer from the beginning, and does not stand in the truth because there is no truth in him. Whenever he speaks a lie, he speaks from his own nature, for he is a liar and the father of lies* (John 8:44).

The *Great Exchange* took place. Adam and Eve exchanged being one with God, and they exchanged fathers. They lost their, and our, identity as children of God. The great mission of the second Adam, Jesus Christ, was to restore those who put their trust in Him back into the family of God and their identity as His children.

The *Great Exchange* took place based on judgment and accusation. That is, they ate the fruit because they judged what God said, they judged what God intended, and they judged God's motive. Not only that, but they also condemned themselves and mankind to a life of judgment and accusation. This is evidenced by their first responses. They judged themselves: "we were naked." They judged God: "we were afraid of You." They judged others (she made me do it): "the woman You gave me." They judged that they knew better than God, as they saw something was lacking—*we don't know good from evil*—and decided it was up to them to get it.

At this point, two things happened. The first was that sin entered the world.

The *Merriam-Webster Dictionary* defines sin as "an offense against religious or moral law; an action that is or is felt to be highly reprehensible; an often serious shortcoming; transgression of the law of God; and, a vitiated state of human nature in which the self is estranged from God."[2]

There are elements of truth within this definition. However, when sin is associated and constructed within a religious framework, a performance-driven culture is established. Then a "right and wrong" paradigm defines a person's identity. For example, if I do not sin—do the wrong thing—I am loved and considered a good person. However, if I do sin, I am considered a bad person—a sinner.

As a result, the concept of sin is tied to a set of religious *dos and don'ts*. Whereas sin ought to be considered and understood within a relational framework. Sin is a real issue, and I believe we will all one day stand before the Judge and be judged (see 2 Cor. 5:10; Rom. 14:12). I am pointing to the thought that sin is less about "right and wrong" based on a set of religious ideologies. It is more about being in right relationship with God, others, ourselves, and creation. Sinning involves attitudes and behaviors that create division in the relationship between God and us, each other, ourselves, and creation. Sin is a barrier to flourishing and whole relationships. As an enemy of God, sin destroys His perfect plan for the created order.

Sin is more than breaking the law and being disobedient. Sin results in the dividing of relationships and stops us from truly knowing the Father. Sin eclipses the truth of who the Father is, and as a result we project our own brokenness onto the Father.

If sin was only a matter of legality, then to make things right God could organize a legal solution to cover humanity's sin. While this view is "consistent with the mythology of the fallen mind," it does not address the crux of the issue! The reality of Jesus' birth, life, death, and resurrection were not to fulfill some legal contract so that we might behave appropriately, giving us a ticket into some ethereal place called heaven! No, the reality of Jesus points us to the good Father. That we might know the Father through Jesus and, as a result, be free from the darkness of the fallen mind and of wrong belief.

The beliefs we hold about God, ourselves, and others will influence how we respond to the presence of sin in our lives. When responding to sin, we must look past the symptomatic behavior and attempt to identify and correct the wrong beliefs.

Christopher Marshall expounds on righteousness as the relational working out of just relations:

> The biblical notion of righteousness refers broadly to doing, being, declaring, or bringing about what is right. Righteousness is a comprehensively relational reality. It is not a private moral attribute one has on one's own. It

is something that inheres in our relationships as social beings. To be righteous is to be true to the demands of a relationship, whether that relationship is with God or with other persons.[3]

The second thing that happened when Adam and Eve exchanged oneness with God for being like God was that they exercised their lordship over the Lordship of God.

We have been made in the image of God. He has a Kingdom. God created us to rule over and subdue a domain—the earth. He also gave us a free will to exercise in how to rule over and subdue our domain, which includes our lives. So, as God created us in His image, He empowered us to make choices as we rule and subdue the earth and our own lives. That is, we are all lords. The first evidence of this in children is around the age of two. They find the word "no" and the power of a tantrum. Then there is the expression with siblings and friends of "these are my toys," "this is my space," and "you're not my friend anymore." In teenage years, "lordship" can be expressed by such behaviors as open rebellion and withdrawal. Most of us will likely recall our own conduct and attitudes during these years.

God's original intent, as evidenced by having two trees in the garden, is that we would partake of His life—the tree of life. We are to surrender our lordship by not eating from the tree of knowledge of good and evil. Before coming to put our trust in Jesus, we center our lordship on making our own judgments. These are based on thoughts and decisions that are primarily focused on benefiting us. We discover how to rely on ourselves rather than relying on the Lord's all-knowing insights and judgments, thus creating personal and ethnic cultures anchored in judgment.

Where acceptance was freely given by God to Adam and Eve as an expression of oneness, the exchange to knowing good from evil resulted in finding acceptance through the evaluating filter of good and evil. That is, we receive and acquire acceptance, worth, and value on the condition that our knowledge of good and evil approves of behavior. Acceptance is found in performance where we strive to display and acquire all we deem good, and we strive to suppress and avoid all we consider evil.

We see this in Adam and Eve. When their eyes of judgment were opened, fear (hiding from God), shame and condemnation (covering their nakedness), and blame and accusation (defending themselves) dominated how they now related to God, self, and others. That is, they moved from a relationship with God and others with acceptance at its core to a relationship with satan, with judgment expressed based on performance, at their core.

The nature of satan as a father is to make false judgments about everything: *"Whenever he speaks a lie, he speaks from his own nature, for he is a liar and the father of lies"* (John 8:44). He is the father of lies and judgment because he conceived of judgment in himself when he judged he was better than God.

> *How you have fallen from heaven,*
> *O star of the morning, son of the dawn!*
> *You have been cut down to the earth,*
> *You who have weakened the nations!*
> *But you said in your heart,*
> *"I will ascend to heaven;*
> *I will raise my throne above the stars of God,*
> *And I will sit on the mount of assembly*
> *In the recesses of the north.*
> *I will ascend above the heights of the clouds;*
> *I will make myself like the Most High"* (Isaiah 14:12-14).

Oneness Restored and the Consequences

Jesus came preaching the Gospel of the Kingdom of God:

> *Jesus was going throughout all Galilee, teaching in their synagogues and proclaiming the gospel of the kingdom, and healing every kind of disease and every kind of sickness among the people* (Matthew 4:23).

Jesus taught us to pray, "Your Kingdom come."

> *Your kingdom come.*
> *Your will be done,*
> *On earth as it is in heaven* (Matthew 6:10).

I'm wondering whether you have considered what you would see if the Kingdom did come.

Jesus instructed us to seek first His Kingdom.

> *But seek first His kingdom and His righteousness, and all these things will be added to you* (Matthew 6:33).

Again, I'm wondering if you have contemplated what you are looking for when you seek the Kingdom.

Luke tells us that Jesus spent the 40 days after His resurrection and before His ascension talking to the disciples about the Kingdom.

> *To these He also presented Himself alive after His suffering, by many convincing proofs, appearing to them over a period of forty days and speaking of the things concerning the kingdom of God* (Acts 1:3).

Clearly, the knowledge of the Kingdom was very significant to Jesus (see Matt. 13:1-58).

Theologians and church leaders answer the question, "How do we define the Kingdom?" in many different ways. I will offer the following definition: "The Kingdom of God is to be found wherever the supreme rule and reign of Jesus' authority exists." With this in mind, the activity of the Kingdom is to restore everything back to the way God originally intended it to be. This presupposes that the existence of Shalom—the place of flourishing in God's ways—is at the heart of God's redemptive purposes.

Genesis 1:26-27 reveals that God's primary purpose for all mankind and every individual is to be made and to live in the image of God.

> *Then God said, "Let Us make man in Our image, according to Our likeness; and let them rule over the fish of the sea and over the birds of the sky and over the cattle and over all the earth, and over every creeping thing that creeps on the earth." God created man in His own image, in the image of God He created him; male and female He created them* (Genesis 1:26-27).

When Adam and Eve made the great exchange, the image of God in mankind began to die and degrade as people started to take on the image of mankind's substitute father, the devil.

> *Jesus said to them, "If God were your Father, you would love Me, for I proceeded forth and have come from God, for I have not even come on My own initiative, but He sent Me. Why do you not understand what I am saying? It is because you cannot hear My word. You are of your father the devil, and you want to do the desires of your father. He was a murderer from the beginning, and does not stand in the truth because there is no truth in him. Whenever he speaks a lie, he speaks from his own nature, for he is a liar and the father of lies.*

> *But because I speak the truth, you do not believe Me"* (John 8:42-45).

The activity of the Kingdom, through the work of the Spirit and the Word, is to restore everything back to the way God originally intended it to be. One of the key focuses for our transformation is the way we reflect the image of God. The image of God is significantly characterized by Their oneness as evidenced by Their declaration, "Let *Us* make man in Our image," and as represented in the way They are love.

> *Beloved, let us love one another, for love is from God; and everyone who loves is born of God and knows God* (1 John 4:7).

Consequently, our redemption and progress in transformation are empowered by our return to oneness with God and the mystery it represents.

This is why Jesus is Emmanuel, God with us. The outcome of salvation is that Heaven, the Kingdom, enters us: *"For, behold, the Kingdom of God is within you"* (Luke 17:21 KJV); before but not without, enabling us to "go to Heaven" when we die. Thus, Heaven for us is more accurately represented by transformation, not relocation. This is because eternal life is the knowledge of God in Jesus (see John 17:3), which we begin to grow in when we put our trust in Jesus, not something or someplace we step into when we die.

With this in mind, the image of God is restored in us through the journey of discovering our inheritance. Through transformation we will want to join, for ourselves and others, into Paul's prayer:

> *And this I pray, that your love may abound still more and more in real knowledge and all discernment, so that you may approve the things that are excellent, in order to be sincere and blameless until the day of Christ* (Philippians 1:9-10).

Equally, we will pay close attention to Jesus' admonition to not judge:

> *Do not judge so that you will not be judged. For in the way you judge, you will be judged; and by your standard of measure, it will be measured to you. Why do you look at the speck that is in your brother's eye, but do not notice the log that is in your own eye? Or how can you say to your brother, "Let me take the speck out of your eye," and behold, the log is in your own eye? You hypocrite, first take the log out of your own eye, and then you will see clearly to take the speck out of your brother's eye* (Matthew 7:1-5).

Greg Boyd begins his book *Repenting of Religion* by appropriately observing:

> "We love only insofar as we abstain from judgment. Love is the central command in Scripture and judgment the central prohibition."[4]

Where judgment broke our oneness with God, love restored our oneness with God.

> *For God so loved the world, that He gave His only begotten Son, that whoever believes in Him shall not perish, but have eternal life. For God did not send the Son into the world to judge the world, but that the world might be saved through Him* (John 3:16-17).

Here Jesus explicitly contrasts love and judgment as He did not come to judge.

Our restoration into oneness with God is powerfully illustrated by the story we know as the prodigal son. The father is actually the central character in this story. Luke 15:20 tells us:

> *So he got up and came to his father. But while he was still a long way off, his father saw him and felt compassion for him, and ran and embraced him and kissed him.*

It was compassion, love in action, which motivated the Father's patience, excitement, and embracing of this wayward son back into the family, back into oneness through a complete restoration. No questions asked. No guilt—the prodigal didn't even get to give his rehearsed repentance speech. No shame or condemnation from the father because compassion is our only appropriate response to sin.

> *For judgment will be merciless to one who has shown no mercy; mercy triumphs over judgment* (James 2:13).
>
> *Above all, keep fervent in your love for one another, because love covers a multitude of sins* (1 Peter 4:8).

On the other hand, the older brother is still captive to the consequences of judgment that come from oneness being broken. He, like most of us at times, has not fully grasped that in His father's house love, compassion, and the restoration of oneness are the supreme values.

Even when Adam and Eve sinned, God's compassion and mercy were evident. His love covered their sin by providing garments to cover their felt need of nakedness. He did not storm into the Garden motivated by anger that offered accusations and punishment. Instead, He entered asking questions to enable self-awareness and personal responsibility to open the door to repentance. The first question, "Where are you?" was not geographical in intent. He knew where they were; God is all-knowing, omniscient. He was asking where they were relationally, hoping their self-awareness would result in an acknowledgment of their sin and a desire to set things right. However, their response was that they were afraid of the One who had always shown them love and kindness.

God's second question, "Who told you that?" was motivated by a desire for an honest conversation to lead to the door being opened through personal responsibility for their sin, resulting in forgiveness and some level of restoration. He was offering mercy and compassion.

Even in their banishment, He was acting with mercy. If they were to eat from the tree of life, then mankind would have become immortal with sin at our core. So Adam and Eve were removed from the Garden by God as He knew that He would send a second Adam, Jesus, to restore oneness.

Father God never wanted to be a judge. The role of judges in western culture includes protecting the integrity of things. For example, a thief is placed in jail to protect the integrity of the possessions others own. A rapist is jailed to protect the integrity and well-being of women. Father God had to protect the integrity of eternal life with Him. If Adam and Eve had eaten from the tree of life, then sin would have been eternally locked up in the heart of all mankind.

Jesus is the way, the truth, and *the life* (see John 14:16). The tree of life in the Garden represents Jesus. Jesus had to live a sinless life to pay the penalty for our sin in His death so that when we placed our trust in Him we would receive eternal life. With the important result that we were not just declared "not guilty." Instead, we were declared innocent as all our sins—past, present, and future—have been forgiven.

> *When you were dead in your transgressions and the uncircumcision of your flesh, He made you alive together with Him, having forgiven us all our transgressions* (Colossians 2:13).
>
> *Namely, that God was in Christ reconciling the world to Himself, not counting their trespasses against them, and He has committed to us the word of reconciliation* (2 Corinthians 5:19).

> *Every priest stands daily ministering and offering time after time the same sacrifices, which can never take away sins; but He, having offered one sacrifice for sins for all time, sat down at the right hand of God* (Hebrews 10:11-12).
>
> *Now where there is forgiveness of these things, there is no longer any offering for sin* (Hebrews 10:18).

Equally, while Jesus came to save and judge, His death and resurrection resulted in Him being the only one who can judge our eternal state for which He paid the price.

> *For not even the Father judges anyone, but He has given all judgment to the Son* (John 5:22).

When we neglect our choice to not put our trust in Jesus—who was punished for all our sin—then instead of our punishment being placed on Jesus as our substitute it is placed on us personally. Jesus is the only one who now is perfectly positioned to make this call.

The net result is that Father God has been restored to being a Father only and has released the role of judgment for sin to Jesus. Allow me to illustrate the importance of this knowledge using a true story from my relationship with my son David. (He has given me permission to use this example.)

When David was fifteen, like all of us, he was searching to understand, "Who am I?; Why am I here?; and Where do I fit?" His journey of discovery took him to a place of stealing phones from his classmates at school as a subconscious way of defining himself outside of the pressures of being a pastor's kid. He was caught, and the school staff rang our home to inform my wife, Lyn.

I arrived home, knowing I was cooking a barbeque dinner that night. Lyn explained what she had been told, and we were not really sure how we would manage the consequences for our son. I asked Lyn to give me five minutes at the barbeque to pray about the appropriate response and to then send Davey to see me.

As I was walking to the barbeque, I felt the Lord say to me, "Do you want to be his father or his judge?"

I already knew the truth that behavior is always the echo of belief. For example, should you ever behave in an angry way it will always be because of what you believe at the time. That is, if you think you are being mistreated, being accused of something you disagree with, or being threatened the belief elicits a behavioral response from you. Behavior is always the echo of belief.

So David believed something that was manifested in his behavior of stealing. Father God came into the Garden of Eden asking Adam and Eve questions: "Where are you?" and "Who told you that?" for the purpose of self-awareness and personal responsibility. I could now be a father by asking Davey questions to promote self-awareness and personal responsibility regarding what he was believing. Alternatively, I could be a judge and simply punish him for the behavior of stealing. I recognized he needed to suffer the consequences and pay the price for his poor behavior. However, I understood the Lord was leading me to allow the school to be his judge, and I would be his father.

In this instance, the role of being a father was to help Davey find freedom from the power of the *lies* he believed about who he was and how he fitted in life. My role was to be a guide who showed him who I thought he was in Christ through my eyes of affection and belief in who he really was. As a guide, I was also positioned to hold him accountable for what he believed as he matured and developed.

We are now the best of friends because I responded as a father. However, if I had positioned myself as a judge, I could have put him through the resentment of being misunderstood, not known, and not heard. We found a place of oneness together. Davey is an outstanding man who loves Jesus, is serving Him brilliantly, and is a great husband and father.

As followers of Jesus, we have been adopted into the family of God. That family is the Father, Son, and Holy Spirit. All other members of the family of God are adopted members of the family. As adopted members, we experience their oneness. We are invited to live in and through the values of their oneness.

> *I do not ask on behalf of these alone, but for those also who believe in Me through their word; that they may all be one; even as You, Father, are in Me and I in You, that they also may be in Us, so that the world may believe that You sent Me* (John 17:20-21).
>
> *The glory which You have given Me I have given to them, that they may be one, just as We are one; I in them and You in Me, that they may be perfected in unity, so that the world may know that You sent Me, and loved them, even as You have loved Me. Father, I desire that they also, whom You have given Me, be with Me where I am, so that they may see My glory which You have given Me, for You loved Me before the foundation of the world* (John 17:22-24).

These values are found in a life together that is given to being others-centered, vulnerable, meek, humble, serving, blessing, honoring, faithful, and always exhibiting the fruit of the Spirit. The overarching value is, *"The glory which you have given Me I have given to them"* (John 17:22). The original Greek word here for "glory" means "to offer a personal opinion that gives value." That is, we always honor the image of God (*imago Dei*) in others.

As we make disciples and are being made into disciples through relationship, we are to guide one another to wholeness and transformation opportunities through commentary on what is seen, not a criticism of what is done. Similarly, we are to offer an observation, not judgment. We all need help to see what we can't see and to know what we don't know. Others see what our hearts know, but our head does not understand in the way we respond and react. The heart of the matter is always a matter of the heart. We all need fathers and mothers who, through love, help us to walk with God, not through judgment.

How do we posture ourselves and be those who offer personal opinions that give value?

A great place to begin is an embrace of the life that prioritizes reconciled diversity. That is, rather than approaching disagreements through a binary lens of right and wrong, we adopt a posture of being reconciled to the fact that we all only know and see in part. Consequently, for example, I am reconciled to the reality that there are lovers of Jesus who believe all miracles ceased with the biblical apostles—cessationists. I do not personally hold this view. However, with a value of reconciled diversity, I can step away from the need to correct others through judgment. Instead, we adopt a desire to know how they have reached their conclusion. I posture myself away from telling for the purpose of agreement. I see unity, oneness, powerfully pursued and expressed through reconciled diversity, not uniformity. I exchange being right (in my opinion) for offering personal opinions that give value. I hold convictions and execute them with kindness, compassion, and care. I choose to not polarize people but help them find one another's value and worth as God's creation. I hear their story, not win the argument.

These postures can be challenging when our understanding of adoption into a family is one of inclusion rather than restoration. I have had the privilege of observing numbers of families choose to adopt older children. The adopted child comes with their own life experiences and personal culture. They are included, not restored, because they have no relationship to the experience of their adopted family. Culturally, we are more attuned to viewing adoption as a process of inclusion, not restoration. Restoration calls out of us something present in us that originated with where we are being restored to. Restoration is a process that brings alive what was lost.

These ideas are illustrated by contrasting the perspectives of the salvation experience as "Am I a sinner saved by grace or am I a child of God?" Being a sinner saved by grace, I am still included in the family of God but exhibiting some level of deficiency. Being a child of God means old things have passed away, and I have been restored fully into the person I was always meant to be. That is a new creation and the righteousness of God.

> *He made Him who knew no sin to be sin on our behalf, so that we might become the righteousness of God in Him* (2 Corinthians 5:21).

When God's people see adoption as *inclusion* they tend to live from a "try harder," works and performance posture in their spirituality. When God's people view adoption as *restoration*, they live from a stance of empowered grace and acceptance in their spirituality.

The story found in Second Kings 9:1-13 of Mephibosheth's relationship with David illustrates the essential need for the people of God to correctly view the restorative power represented in their adoption into God's family.

The context of these verses is important. Saul had been the king, and his son Jonathan was next in line. However, David had been anointed by God, through Samuel, to be the future king. Yet Jonathan and David were best friends. As it turned out, Saul and Jonathan died together in battle, making way for David and his heirs to ascend to the throne.

Culturally, when a new bloodline ascended to the throne, the new king killed all the remaining descendants of the previous king. This was to ensure their right to the throne was not challenged in the future. Jonathan's son Mephibosheth was in danger of being killed. So his nurse attempted to carry him to a hiding place and safety, yet in the process dropped Mephibosheth, who in turn suffered injuries that made him a cripple.

Fast forward many years, and David now wanted to show kindness to anyone left of the house of Saul—that is, the house of his enemies. This has echoes of:

> *Or do you think lightly of the riches of His kindness and tolerance and patience, not knowing that the kindness of God leads you to repentance?* (Romans 2:4)
>
> *For if while we were enemies we were reconciled to God through the death of His Son, much more, having been reconciled, we shall be saved by His life* (Romans 5:10).

Ziba indicated that Jonathan's son, who was a cripple, was still alive, so David asked for him to be brought to David's household. Here David chose someone who had nothing to offer him. Mephibosheth had no wealth and couldn't fight for David in his army. Again, this echoes the fact that God chose us; we did not choose Him. When God chose us, we were broken and had nothing to offer Him except our love and trust.

David then declared his intent to Mephibosheth. Through kindness, he was going to restore all of Mephibosheth's inheritance and all he was familiar with, as well as being counted as a member of the royal family. Mephibosheth was unable to comprehend this honor and could only see himself as a "dead dog." This has echoes of us not being able to see past being "sinners saved by grace" who are at best included in the life of the royal household.

The story concludes with, "so Mephibosheth ate at David's table as one of the king's sons." His destiny, through Jonathan, was to be the son of the king. David restored his destiny, just as Jesus has restored us:

> *But you are a chosen race, a royal priesthood, a holy nation, a people for God's own possession, so that you may proclaim the excellencies of Him who has called you out of darkness into His marvelous light; for you once were not a people, but now you are the people of God; you had not received mercy, but now you have received mercy* (1 Peter 2:9-10).

You have not just been included into God's family—you have been restored.

There is a vast difference.

Our restoration as adopted children of God is from a love that acts unconditionally, ascribing worth to another at a cost to self. We are not only to be the recipients of this love that God has poured out upon us. We are also to be participants in the love the Father, Son, and Holy Spirit have for one another, for us, and for others. This is why John takes time to so thoroughly explore his proposition:

> *Beloved, let us love one another, for love is from God; and everyone who loves is born of God and knows God* (1 John 4:7).

Summary

As followers of Jesus, there is a mystery that Christ dwells in us through the Holy Spirit who is our counselor, helper, and comforter.

We have been adopted into oneness with God and have a new identity as children of God accompanied by a staggering inheritance.

God became what we are so that we might become what He is.

We are to learn through a relational process of transformation to live and walk with God from a place of abiding in Him.

The consequences of the loss of our oneness in God are:

- an exchange of fathers
- the entrance of judgment
- the need to understand sin in the context of relationship before but not without behavior
- the elevation of the way people express their lordship

As the second Adam, Jesus came to:

- restore oneness and relationship with God as Father, not judge
- express redemptive love and replace judgment with compassion
- establish the Kingdom in and through followers of Jesus

We need to embrace and demonstrate the lifestyle and power of reconciled diversity.

Reflection

1. How does the mystery that Christ dwells in you impact the way you live daily?
2. Can you identify three ways you regularly judge others or yourself?
3. In each of the above areas of judgment, what would a compassionate response look like? Follow up by asking Holy Spirit to help you become that person.
4. What is one area in your life where you exercise "your lordship" and what would Holy Spirit say to you about that?
5. What stops you from living in reconciled diversity with *all* others who follow Jesus?

Notes

1. Beliefnet, "Step up to God's Banquet Table," https://www.beliefnet.com/inspiration/christian-inspiration/2004/11/step-up-to-gods-banquet-table.aspx.
2. *Merriam-Webster Dictionary*, s.v. "Sin," https://www.merriam-webster.com/dictionary/sin.
3. Chris Marshall, "Divine Justice as Restorative Justice," Center for Christian Ethics, (2012) http://www.baylor.edu/content/services/document.php/163072.pdf.
4. Boyd, *Repenting of Religion*, 9.

Chapter Two

The Greater Commandment

...Restored by and to His Love

The movie *Hacksaw Ridge* recounts the remarkable life story of Desmond Doss.

Raised as a child in the 1920s in rural Virginia with a Seventh-Day Adventist faith, Desmond nearly killed his little brother Hal while playing. After the Japanese attack on Pearl Harbor, Desmond enlisted in the army as a combat medic. He was placed into basic training under the command of Sergeant Howell. While he excelled physically, he remained true to his faith expression of refusing to handle a gun. He believed in the commandment, "Thou shall not kill," and refused to train on Saturdays as it was his Sabbath.

Howell and Captain Glover, who was Sergeant Howell's officer in command of basic training, attempted to discharge Desmond for psychiatric reasons under Section 8. They were overruled, as Desmond's religious beliefs did not constitute mental illness. They subsequently continued to torment him by putting him through grueling labor, intending to get him to leave of his own accord. Despite being beaten one night by his fellow soldiers, he refused to identify his attackers and continued training.

Desmond's unit was assigned to the 77th Infantry Division and deployed to the Pacific. During the Battle of Okinawa, Desmond's unit was informed that they were to relieve the 96th Infantry Division, which was tasked with ascending and securing the Maeda Escarpment ("Hacksaw Ridge"). During the initial fight, with heavy losses on both sides, Desmond saved the life of his squad mate Smitty, earning his respect. As the Americans camped for the night, Desmond revealed to Smitty that his aversion to holding a firearm stemmed from nearly shooting his drunken father, who threatened his mother with a gun. Smitty apologized for doubting his courage, and the two reconciled.

The next morning, the Japanese launched a massive counterattack and drove the Americans off the escarpment. Smitty was killed, while Howell and several of Desmond's squad mates were left injured on the battlefield. Desmond heard the cries of dying soldiers and returned to save them, carrying the wounded to the cliff's edge and belaying them down by rope, each time praying to save one more. The arrival of dozens of wounded, once presumed dead, was a shock to the rest of the unit below. When day broke, Desmond rescued Howell and the two escaped from Hacksaw under enemy fire.

Captain Glover apologized for dismissing Desmond's beliefs as "cowardice" and stated that they were scheduled to retake the ridge on Saturday but would not launch the next attack without him. Desmond agreed, but the operation was delayed until after he concluded his Sabbath prayers. With reinforcements, they turned the tide of battle. In an ambush set by Japanese soldiers feigning surrender, Desmond managed to save Glover and others by deflecting enemy grenades. Desmond was eventually wounded by a grenade, but the battle was won. Desmond descended the cliff, clutching the Bible his wife gave him.

Desmond's inspirational life reflects heroism motivated by extraordinary compassion and love based on his relationship with Jesus.

The Greater Commandment

Jesus made love the central focus of Christian spirituality when he rewrote the second of the two great commandments of the Old Testament. He established a *new* way for God's people who put their trust in Jesus. No longer are God's people to love one another *as they love themselves*. Instead, in John 13:34-35, Jesus promises:

> *A new commandment I give to you, that you love one another,* **even as I have loved you**, *that you also love one another. By this all men will know that you are My disciples, if you have love for one another.*

Jesus reaffirms that for God's people to move forward into the future they are to know the height, breadth, length, and depth of His love. They now need to be motivated, established, and expressed from this new platform (see Eph. 3:17-19).

> *This is My commandment, that you love one another, just as I have loved you* (John 15:12).

Jesus has introduced the greater commandment for New Testament living. His introduction of the greater commandment can be clearly understood, and is to be expected, in light of Hebrews 7:12 and 18-19.

> *For when the priesthood is changed, of necessity there takes place a change of law also.*
> *...For, on the one hand, there is a setting aside of a former commandment because of its weakness and uselessness* (for the Law made nothing perfect), *and on the other hand there is a bringing in of a better hope, through which we draw near to God.*

Before going any further, join me on a significant diversion. The writer of Hebrews goes further with these thoughts when he writes:

> *When He said, "A new covenant," He has made the first obsolete. But whatever is becoming obsolete and growing old is ready to disappear* (Hebrews 8:13).

Here I need to briefly speak to our relationship with the old covenant Law as it is crucial to understand in the context of how we make and become disciples.

What did Jesus say about the Law?

First, He said the whole Law and Prophets (note, this is the Old Testament) depend on two commandments:

> *But when the Pharisees heard that Jesus had silenced the Sadducees, they gathered themselves together. One of them, a lawyer, asked Him a question, testing Him, "Teacher, which is the great commandment in the Law?" And He said to him, "'You shall love the Lord your God with all your heart, and with all your soul, and with all your mind.' This is the great and foremost commandment. The second is like it, 'You shall love your neighbor as yourself.' On these two commandments depend the whole Law and the Prophets"* (Matthew 22:34-40).

Second, He said He came to fulfill, not abolish, the Law and Prophets.

> *Do not think that I came to abolish the Law or the Prophets; I did not come to abolish but to fulfill* (Matthew 5:17).

Third, He said that the Law will last for the history of creation until it is accomplished.

> *For truly I say to you, until heaven and earth pass away, not the smallest letter or stroke shall pass from the Law until all is accomplished* (Matthew 5:18).

Fourth, He said if we annul the commandments, we will be the least in the Kingdom, and if we keep and teach them we shall be great in the Kingdom.

> *Whoever then annuls one of the least of these commandments, and teaches others to do the same, shall be called least in the kingdom of heaven; but whoever keeps and teaches them, he shall be called great in the kingdom of heaven* (Matthew 5:19).

So how do we reconcile the thoughts from Hebrews that the Law is weak, useless, and obsolete with these teachings from Jesus?

The answer lies in the way the Law and the Prophets are used to influence the way we live and define spiritual maturity. The Pharisees and Sadducees used the Law to describe and assess righteousness. The Books of Romans and Galatians in particular are Paul's great defense that righteousness is not based on keeping the Law but rather through faith in Jesus Christ.

> *because by the works of the Law no flesh will be justified in His sight; for through the Law comes the knowledge of sin* (Romans 3:20).

> *nevertheless knowing that a man is not justified by the works of the Law but through faith in Christ Jesus, even we have believed in Christ Jesus, so that we may be justified by faith in Christ and not by the works of the Law; since by the works of the Law no flesh will be justified.* (Galatians 2:16).

And again, in Philippians Paul writes:

> *and may be found in Him, not having a righteousness of my own derived from the Law, but that which is through faith in Christ, the righteousness which comes from God on the basis of faith* (Philippians 3:9).

For the Jews, their lives and spiritual maturity were defined and assessed through how well they performed in following the Law. It is this use of the Law and Prophets that was weak, useless, as well as now being obsolete.

So how are we to live with God and reveal His Kingdom as followers of Jesus? Love has always been the central feature of both the old and new covenants. However, the basis of how we love and from where has changed. It has moved from "as we love ourselves" to "as I have loved you." When the Law is used to define and assess right standing with God (righteousness), love appears to be given by God, and received by us, on the basis or performance. When I do what is right, I receive love. When I do what is wrong, love is withdrawn. This way of giving and receiving love is strongly echoed in the way we experience love from our parents, siblings, families, and others. Consequently, we love ourselves (and others) through the lens of performance, while Jesus loves us through the lens of acceptance.

> *Blessed be the God and Father of our Lord Jesus Christ, who has blessed us with every spiritual blessing in the heavenly places in Christ, just as He chose us in Him before the foundation of the world, that we would be holy and blameless before Him. In love He predestined us to adoption as sons through Jesus Christ to Himself, according to the kind intention of His will, to the praise of the glory of His grace, which He freely bestowed on us in the Beloved. In Him we have redemption through His blood, the forgiveness of our trespasses, according*

to the riches of His grace which He lavished on us. In all wisdom and insight He made known to us the mystery of His will, according to His kind intention which He purposed in Him (Ephesians 1:3-9).

This profound difference in how to live with God and reveal His Kingdom is illustrated in the following table.

KINGDOM THROUGH OLD TESTAMENT EYES	KINGDOM THROUGH NEW TESTAMENT EYES
Gospel of demand	Gospel of invitation
Behavior management	Belief management
Make people better	Make people different
Self-love	Love of Christ
Performance	Acceptance

When the Gospel is presented through an Old Testament lens, it is often communicated as a "closed system." That is, God's Kingdom is defined by the rules that need to be followed to keep you in the Kingdom. These rules create boundaries that provide evidence that you are in or out. In this closed system, the way in is through Jesus. However, once in you need to perform to belong, and there is the overarching sense that God's favor and blessing are earned through good behavior.

When the Gospel is presented through a New Testament lens, it is communicated as a "centered system." That is, God's Kingdom is defined by grace and mercy that empower us to live like Jesus as we progressively surrender to His love for us and others. Jesus brought people into the Kingdom through invitation. To the disciples: "Come follow Me, and I will make you…." To the woman caught in adultery: "Neither do I condemn you. Go your way and sin no more." As they, and we, respond to the invitation to experience His love, He expects us to change our way and behavior to His higher standard. That is, "Love one another as I have loved you." We become centered in, nourished by, and motivated from His love for us and our experience of that love.

The paradox for our understanding of love and righteousness is that we, as followers of Jesus, are called to a higher standard of behavior—because of the love that we have received and can experience with Jesus—while not being loved and valued based on behavior. For example:

> *You have heard that the ancients were told, "You shall not commit murder" and "Whoever commits murder shall be liable to the court." But I say to you that everyone who is angry with his brother shall be guilty before the court; and whoever says to his brother, "You good-for-nothing," shall be guilty before the supreme court; and whoever says, "You fool," shall be guilty enough to go into the fiery hell* (Matthew 5:21-22).
>
> *You have heard that it was said, "You shall not commit adultery"; but I say to you that everyone who looks at a woman with lust for her has already committed adultery with her in his heart* (Matthew 5:27-28).
>
> *You have heard that it was said, "You shall love your neighbor and hate your enemy." But I say to you, love your enemies and pray for those who persecute you* (Matthew 5:43-44).

Because we are loved by the Trinity in the same way They love one another, we are to live in Their light as They train us in righteousness—that is, being loyal to the demands of building and maintaining the relationship. We are not expected to do the behaviors above from Matthew 5. We are called to *abide*—that is, to *be* in Him so that His love for us and in us flows through us. His love empowers our desire to be like Him and believe we are now in Him so that we behave like Him. Behavior is always the echo of belief.

Dallas Willard, in *The Divine Conspiracy*, has profoundly helpful insights here when he writes:

> To be sure, law is not the source of rightness, but it is forever the course of rightness…The law of God marks the movements of God's kingdom, of his own actions and of how the kingdom works. When we keep the law, we step into his ways and drink in his power.[1]

That is because the law is the course of righteousness; there is *Law* in the Kingdom of God that is like the natural *Law* of gravity in that it is immutable and never changes.

Using gravity as an illustration, it is a *law* of the natural world. We all know it, in turn, generates other laws, such as, if a person steps off the roof of a two-story building, they will sustain physical damage. Accordingly, governments create occupational health and safety rules to protect workers from being unnecessarily injured through poor work practices.

What is a *Law* of the Kingdom of God that, like gravity, is immutable and never changes?

My firm conviction is that it is *oneness*.

The nature and character of the Godhead are founded in their oneness.

> *Then God said, "Let Us make man in Our image, according to Our likeness; and let them rule over the fish of the sea and over the birds of the sky and over the cattle and over all the earth, and over every creeping thing that creeps on the earth"* (Genesis 1:26).
>
> *Therefore Jesus answered and was saying to them, "Truly, truly, I say to you, the Son can do nothing of Himself, unless*

> *it is something He sees the Father doing; for whatever the Father does, these things the Son also does in like manner"* (John 5:19).
>
> *That they may all be one; even as You, Father, are in Me and I in You, that they also may be in Us, so that the world may believe that You sent Me* (John 17:21).
>
> *But when He, the Spirit of truth, comes, He will guide you into all the truth; for He will not speak on His own initiative, but whatever He hears, He will speak; and He will disclose to you what is to come. He will glorify Me, for He will take of Mine and will disclose it to you. All things that the Father has are Mine; therefore I said that He takes of Mine and will disclose it to you* (John 16:13-15).

Early church fathers used the term *perichoresis* to describe how the Godhead—Father, Son, and Holy Spirit—danced together. It relates to how they move as one with precision and fluidity to create meaningful work together. That is, the divine relationship focuses each member of the Trinity on each other and on us. It also refers to how the Godhead interacts with all of creation.

> *For by Him all things were created, both in the heavens and on earth, visible and invisible, whether thrones or dominions or rulers or authorities—all things have been created through Him and for Him. He is before all things, and in Him all things hold together* (Colossians 1:16-17).

As it is with the *law* of gravity, so it is with the *Law* of the Kingdom of God. That is, in the world of the Spirit, there are unavoidable consequences if we ignore the place of being *one* with God and man.

> *For God so loved the world, that He gave His only begotten Son, that whoever believes in Him shall not perish, but have eternal life* (John 3:16).

> *Now the deeds of the flesh are evident, which are: immorality, impurity, sensuality, idolatry, sorcery, enmities, strife, jealousy, outbursts of anger, disputes, dissensions, factions, envying, drunkenness, carousing, and things like these, of which I forewarn you, just as I have forewarned you, that those who practice such things will not inherit the kingdom of God* (Galatians 5:19-21).

Accordingly, the Lord gave us laws, such as the Ten Commandments, to show us that breaking *oneness* will result in spiritual, social, and psychological harm. Conversely, keeping laws will result in us experiencing oneness with God, others, and ourselves. Next, the lawyers of the Old Testament created rules to ostensibly protect us further.

Dallas Willard is again extraordinarily insightful when he writes:

> He knows that we cannot keep the law by trying to keep the law. To succeed in keeping the law one must aim at something other and something more. One must aim to become the kind of person from whom the deeds of the law naturally flow…It is the inner life of the soul that we must aim to transform and then behavior will naturally and easily flow.[2]

Jesus described it like this:

> *For there is no good tree which produces bad fruit, nor, on the other hand, a bad tree which produces good fruit. For each tree is known by its own fruit. For men do not gather figs from thorns, nor do they pick grapes from a briar bush. The good man out of the good treasure of his heart brings forth what is good; and the evil man out of the evil treasure brings forth what is evil; for his mouth speaks from that which fills his heart* (Luke 6:43-45).

As we reflect on how the Old Testament affects how we walk in love, it must be remembered that the covenant with Moses was a national covenant, not a personal covenant. That is, it was a covenant between God and the nation of Israel, not God and individuals. Which leads to the thought that the Bible is all God's Word to somebody but is not all of God's Word to everybody. The Word of God is equally inspired, just not similarly applicable.

Let me illustrate. Hang in with me here.

The writers of the New Testament used four different approaches in their writings when engaging with the Law, the Prophets, and the Old Covenant as they looked back through the finished work of the cross. First, there were aspects of the Law that Jesus fulfilled, that is, brought to a designated end. For example, there are now no animal sacrifices required for the forgiveness of sin. It was always God's intent from the beginning that His covenant with Israel was for a set period.

Second, there were aspects of the Law that the New Testament writers viewed as being modified by the finished work of the cross. For example, the Sabbath day was no longer regarded as being Saturday (see Rom. 14:4-6; Heb. 4:8-10). Equally, the second of the two great commandments of the Old Testament was brought to an end as Jesus rewrote it.

Third, some aspects of the Law in the New Testament living have been amplified. Anger is now like murder, lust for a woman is like adultery, etc.

Finally, some aspects of the old covenant remained unchanged, such as honoring your father and mother.

The Jews expected the Messiah to extend something from the Old Testament. However, He came to start something new. Jesus is not an extension of the Old Testament. He acknowledged the past relationship God had with the Jews while laying the groundwork for what was to come. Jesus called His followers to be centered on His new commandment, not the old.

The Old Testament is profoundly helpful in teaching us so much about the nature and character of God. It is full of wisdom from above to help us live successfully and righteously—that is, the course of rightness. It is an excellent guide as to how to walk with God through the journey of life and how to posture our hearts in the varied life experiences we face.

However, with all the above in mind, how Jesus asked us to make disciples goes to a whole new level of significance when He offers these instructions:

> *Go therefore and make disciples of all the nations, baptizing them in the name of the Father and the Son and the Holy Spirit, teaching them to observe all that I commanded you; and lo, I am with you always, even to the end of the age* (Matthew 28:19-20).

The Word "I"

When making disciples, Jesus says, *"teaching them to observe all that I commanded you."* In light of the above, the word "I" here is incredibly significant and is reinforced by Jesus' own words:

> *A new commandment **I give to you*** (John 13:34).
> *This is **My** commandment* (John 15:12).

Jesus maintains that He has His own commandment and at the same time draws attention to the fact that a change has taken place. Jesus wants to highlight the preeminence of His commandment for New Testament living. That is, *love one another as I have loved you.*

This distinction has profound implications for how we approach what it is to be a disciple. When we love based on how Jesus loved us, it is from a posture of *knowing* how we are loved by Jesus, which results in us becoming like Him. This is the central feature of the New Testament way of living. Alternatively, when we love based on how we love ourselves, it is from a posture of *being* constructed on how we receive love from others, which results in us performing in a prescribed way. This was the central feature of an Old Testament way of living.

It Is a Command

Not only did Jesus use the word "I," but He also used it about what He commanded. Jesus didn't request us to love others just as He loved us. He didn't propose it for our consideration, nor did He offer the opportunity for a discussion and exchange of opinions. As the Lord of lords, He stated a requirement that He expects us to give ourselves to. That is, the priority of our spiritual development is to see, know, and comprehend through experience and encounter, not just head knowledge, how deeply we are loved by God.

Paul understood the significance of discerning what we know through learning and what we know through experience and encounter. Jesus' command cannot be lived out fully through learning, which simply meets the requirement to understand intellectually. Jesus' love needs to be experienced and encountered so that it becomes a reality in our hearts as well as our heads. Paul writes:

> *And to know the love of Christ which surpasses knowledge, that you may be filled up to all the fullness of God* (Ephesians 3:19).

The Greek word here for "to know" means to know through experience and encounter. What we know by experience and encounter lodges in our hearts and our inner world. This surpasses what we know in our heads and our accumulated understanding that is located in our thought life. As a result, we are filled up to the fullness of God through heart knowledge, not just head knowledge.

Jesus has prayed and continues to pray at the right hand of the Father for us to have these encounters.

> *I do not ask on behalf of these alone, but for those also who believe in Me through their word…I in them and You in Me, that they may be perfected in unity, so that the world may know that You sent Me, and loved them, even as You have loved Me…and I have made Your name known to them, and will make it known, so that the love with which You loved Me may be in them, and I in them* (John 17:20,23,26).

We are to posture ourselves continually to have such encounters so that we become, in Him, who we already are through our adoption and inheritance. Greg Boyd says it perfectly when he writes:

> The mandate to love is simply a command to *be who we already are*. We are *in Christ*, so we must put off the *old self* and display the *new self* we already are in Christ by thinking and acting in congruity with it. The reality of our participation in the loving fellowship of the triune God longs for expression, and this longing is only satisfied when our thoughts, words, and actions are in harmony with it.[3]

The Place of "Observe"

Further from Matthew 28:20, Jesus instructed us to *teach them to observe*. We teach many things when we help others to become disciples. We teach on forgiveness, prayer, the fruit of the Spirit, giving, and so much more. However, in Jesus' instruction, He asked us to remain focused on one core teaching.

I imagine this practice to be represented by a bicycle wheel with a hub and spokes. All our teachings are to be viewed as spokes that find their connection to the hub of "love one another as I have loved you."

The original Greek word here for "observe" means "to guard from loss by keeping your eye upon." So Jesus wants us to make disciples through teaching that ensures God's people guard from loss by keeping their eye upon how much they are loved by Jesus so that they love others as He loves them.

When you squeeze an orange, you get orange juice. When you squeeze a lemon, you get lemon juice. When you squeeze a Christian, you should get Jesus juice. So when life squeezes you through financial pressure, a negative health diagnosis, failure, discouragement, rejection, and more, do the fruits of the Spirit flow out of you, particularly love? Do such circumstances cause you to take your eye off and lose sight of how much you are loved by God? One of our greatest desires in becoming disciples of Jesus is to overcome those motivations from our inner world that influence us to take our eyes off God's love for us.

In his pursuit of making disciples, Paul became aware of the significance of this principle of "guarding from loss by keeping your eye upon." In the context of desiring that we live with a true knowledge of God and who we are in Christ, Paul offers us a profound insight into how to live through the New Testament commandment.

> *Therefore if you have been raised up with Christ, keep seeking the things above, where Christ is, seated at the right hand of God. Set your mind on the things above, not on the things that are on earth. For you have died and your life is hidden with Christ in God* (Colossians 3:1-3).

I am intrigued by how the broader Body of Christ has theologically taken their eye off the New Testament commandment, instead remaining focused on the two great commandments of the Old Testament. The early church faced the challenge of communicating sound doctrine to an overwhelmingly illiterate culture, leading to the establishment of the Apostle's Creed and Nicene Creed to stabilize and communicate theology. In both these creeds, they quote the two Old Testament commandments but not the new commandment Jesus gave. Similarly, many centuries later, the Westminster Confession and Heidelberg Catechism both refer to the two great commandments of the Old Testament and not Jesus' new commandment. It is also true that the overwhelming majority of preachers and authors rely on the two great commandments of the Old Testament when teaching on love and how to live a life of love.

"Abide" and the New Testament Writers

In John 15, Jesus shows the significance of "guarding from loss by keeping your eye upon" as He explores the place and power of abiding. The Greek word for "abide" means "to remain." Jesus assures us that fruitfulness, answered prayer, and joy are found in abundance when we *remain* in Him and His love. The knowledge that we're friends who are loved, chosen, and appointed provides us with confidence that we are empowered to make the choices to remain. However, we can choose to not remain, risking consequences. Through self-awareness and personal responsibility, we can discover the triggers that distract us from living as a much-loved child.

> *But in all these things we overwhelmingly conquer through Him who loved us. For I am convinced that neither death, nor life, nor angels, nor principalities, nor things present, nor things to come, nor powers, nor height, nor depth, nor any other created thing, will be able to separate us from the love of God, which is in Christ Jesus our Lord* (Romans 8:37-39).

The writers of the New Testament were totally committed to living a lifestyle around God's love. Beginning with Paul:

> *But the goal of our instruction is love from a pure heart and a good conscience and a sincere faith* (1 Timothy 1:5).
>
> *And this I pray, that your love may abound still more and more in real knowledge and all discernment, so that you may approve the things that are excellent, in order to be sincere and blameless until the day of Christ; having been filled with the fruit of righteousness which comes through Jesus Christ, to the glory and praise of God* (Philippians 1:9-11).
>
> *Now may our God and Father Himself and Jesus our Lord direct our way to you; and may the Lord cause you to increase and abound in love for one another, and for all people, just as we also do for you; so that He may establish your hearts without blame in holiness before our God and Father at the coming of our Lord Jesus with all His saints* (1 Thessalonians 3:11-13).
>
> *We ought always to give thanks to God for you, brethren, as is only fitting, because your faith is greatly enlarged, and the love of each one of you toward one another grows ever greater; therefore, we ourselves speak proudly of you among the churches of God for your perseverance and faith in the midst of all your persecutions and afflictions which you endure* (2 Thessalonians 1:3-4).
>
> *Let all that you do be done in love* (1 Corinthians 16:14).
>
> *For in Christ Jesus neither circumcision nor uncircumcision means anything, but faith working through love* (Galatians 5:6).

Then added to and reinforced by:

> *Above all, keep fervent in your love for one another, because love covers a multitude of sins* (1 Peter 4:8).

> *We know love by this, that He laid down His life for us; and we ought to lay down our lives for the brethren. …This is His commandment, that we believe in the name of His Son Jesus Christ, and love one another, just as He commanded us. The one who keeps His commandments abides in Him, and He in him. We know by this that He abides in us, by the Spirit whom He has given us* (1 John 3:16,23-24).
>
> *Blessed is a man who perseveres under trial; for once he has been approved, he will receive the crown of life which the Lord has promised to those who love Him* (James 1:12).

The New Testament church changed the world with limited, if any, access to the written New Testament. The challenges of the Pharisees and Sadducees reveal a preoccupation with what the Jewish Scriptures said was expected. That is, what do our Scriptures say and what must we *do* to be blessed? That is old covenant thinking. The early church, full of new covenant people who kept their eye on Jesus' commandment, seemed to ask—*What does God's love require of me?* John writes:

> *If someone says, "I love God," and hates his brother, he is a liar; for the one who does not love his brother whom he has seen, cannot love God whom he has not seen* (1 John 4:20).

His reference to "cannot love God" is a reference to opportunity, not ability. That is, to refuse to love another is to forgo the opportunity to love God. We don't love because the Bible tells us to love. We love because the Father has loved us through Jesus.

How Has Jesus Loved Us?

To successfully follow Jesus' greater commandment, it is necessary to grow in our understanding of how Jesus loved us. This is the place and resource from which we are to offer "our" love to others.

To help us to begin to explore this, let me illustrate by breaking down Ephesians 1:3-12:

> *Blessed be the God and Father of our Lord Jesus Christ, who has blessed us with every spiritual blessing in the heavenly places in Christ, just as He chose us in Him before the foundation of the world, that we would be holy and blameless before Him. In love He predestined us to adoption as sons through Jesus Christ to Himself, according to the kind intention of His will, to the praise of the glory of His grace, which He freely bestowed on us in the Beloved. In Him we have redemption through His blood, the forgiveness of our trespasses, according to the riches of His grace which He lavished on us. In all wisdom and insight He made known to us the mystery of His will, according to His kind intention which He purposed in Him with a view to an administration suitable to the fullness of the times, that is, the summing up of all things in Christ, things in the heavens and things on the earth. In Him also we have obtained an inheritance, having been predestined according to His purpose who works all things after the counsel of His will, to the end that we who were the first to hope in Christ would be to the praise of His glory.*

Jesus has loved us as the one "*who has blessed us with every spiritual blessing in the heavenly places.*" That is, Jesus has *empowered* our lives by giving His best to us to be all we have been born to be. Therefore, we are to love others by empowering their progress and development through the journey of life.

Jesus has loved us as the one "*who chose us.*" That is, Jesus consciously and willingly *included* us in His family and lifestyle. Therefore, we love others by compassionately including them through acceptance and refusing to judge, criticize, marginalize, or act with prejudice toward others.

Jesus has loved us as the one who made us *"holy and blameless."* That is, Jesus did for me what I could not do for myself so that I would *imitate* Him. Therefore, we love others by examining our lives to keep growing in representing Jesus well so that others have something to imitate for their well-being.

Jesus has loved us by adopting us *"according to the kind intention of His will."* That is, Jesus established me in His circle of life through a deliberate choice to be *kind*. Therefore, we love others by reciprocating this approach to all others around us. We design a life that seeks to always respond with kindness.

Can you see where this is going? Whatever Jesus did for us, we are to do for others. In fact, He commanded us to live this way. Unsurprisingly, Jesus lived the same way in that He loved others as the Father loved Him.

> *I in them and You in Me, that they may be perfected in unity, so that the world may know that You sent Me, and loved them, even as You have loved Me* (John 17:23).

As well as reflecting on how He has loved us, Jesus prays that we are to be absolutely confident that the Father has as much love for us as He has for His Son.

I deeply and sincerely encourage you to take a "Selah" moment. Pause and reflect on what stops or hinders you from believing you are loved by the Father in the same way and as much as He loves Jesus. Whatever you discover that hinders your acceptance of this truth can now be a place where you ask the Lord to deliver you from the faulty elements of your belief system.

Love's Competitor

Nothing is to compete with, modify, supplement, add to, or compromise loving others as we have been loved by Jesus. The greater commandment is to stand head and shoulders above all else as God's love is free but not duty-free. We cannot love, in a redemptive way, those whom we judge.

> *Do not speak against one another, brethren. He who speaks against a brother or judges his brother, speaks against the law and judges the law; but if you judge the law, you are not a doer of the law but a judge of it. There is only one Lawgiver and Judge, the One who is able to save and to destroy; but who are you who judge your neighbor?* (James 4:11-12)

Jesus ascribes complete and total worth to all while we ascribe limited value to others based on our judgments.

> *But God demonstrates His own love toward us, in that while we were yet sinners, Christ died for us* (Romans 5:8).

The greater commandment to love others as Jesus has loved us is not to be qualified by a pursuit of correct doctrine when it stands above loving others. I hear some say, "But what about telling the truth in love?" (see Eph. 4:15). When truth is the guardian of good and evil, it becomes pharisaical judgment (see Luke 11:42). Truth needs to represent the greater commandment where we are learning to transcend the knowledge of good and evil by living in love. This is called reconciled diversity.

When we judge others—even when it feels justified with intentions and motives to defend "our" truth—we continue to eat from the tree of the knowledge of good and evil, ignoring the upward call of the greater commandment.

> *Do not judge so that you will not be judged. For in the way you judge, you will be judged; and by your standard of measure, it will be measured to you. Why do you look at the speck that is in your brother's eye, but do not notice the log*

> *that is in your own eye? Or how can you say to your brother, "Let me take the speck out of your eye," and behold, the log is in your own eye? You hypocrite, first take the log out of your own eye, and then you will see clearly to take the speck out of your brother's eye* (Matthew 7:1-5).

The word for "judge" here means "to scatter." That is, all judgment separates people. This is the antithesis of what we are called to—a life of offering the unconditional love we have received from Jesus to be one with others (see John 17:20-21). When we judge others, we place ourselves above them. In His humanity, Jesus did not glorify or condemn others; His intent was the exact opposite—to save and set free.

> *For God did not send the Son into the world to judge the world, but that the world might be saved through Him* (John 3:17).
>
> *If anyone hears My sayings and does not keep them, I do not judge him; for I did not come to judge the world, but to save the world* (John 12:47).

Application of judgment is shared between Jesus and the Father. This is based on the finished work of the cross and our choices.

> *For not even the Father judges anyone, but He has given all judgment to the Son* (John 5:22).
>
> *You judge according to the flesh; I am not judging anyone. But even if I do judge, My judgment is true; for I am not alone in it, but I and the Father who sent Me* (John 8:15-16).
>
> *He who rejects Me and does not receive My sayings, has one who judges him; the word I spoke is what will judge him at the last day* (John 12:48).

> *To the general assembly and church of the firstborn who are enrolled in heaven, and to God, the Judge of all, and to the spirits of the righteous made perfect* (Hebrews 12:23).
>
> *There is only one Lawgiver and Judge, the One who is able to save and to destroy; but who are you who judge your neighbor?* (James 4:12)

Paul even went so far as to say:

> *I do not even examine myself* (1 Corinthians 4:3).

Joseph understood that we are not to put ourselves in God's place:

> *But Joseph said to them, "Do not be afraid, for am I in God's place? As for you, you meant evil against me, but God meant it for good in order to bring about this present result, to preserve many people alive. So therefore, do not be afraid; I will provide for you and your little ones." So he comforted them and spoke kindly to them* (Genesis 50:19-21).

Our role is to put ourselves in a place where we believe in and hope for the best in others.

> *[Love] bears all things, believes all things, hopes all things, endures all things* (1 Corinthians 13:7).

Only God knows the complete story of a person's life, and only God can accurately judge.

There is a difference between holding someone accountable and judging them. Equally, it is necessary to discern the impact of a person's destructive approach to themselves or others. This requires a change to remove the danger of harm without judging their motive and intent. Our conclusions about others are to be anchored in their infinite worth and value in the Lord's eyes. We are not to elevate their sin as ours to judge.

Many years ago, I learned this lesson when working as a social worker in a residential facility. Families who were abusing their children were ordered to live there for two weeks. A multidisciplinary team of professionals including doctors, nurses, psychologists, teachers, and social workers were to assess the family to establish how to protect the child/children from further abuse.

A young woman aged 16 from a fourth-generation, welfare-recipient family was admitted with her six-month-old daughter. The daughter had been suffering from colic. After screaming for three days and nights, affording the mother little sleep, it all got too much for mum, who threw the child against a wall, breaking an arm and a leg.

While the mother's behavior was unacceptable, I found it to be understandable. Her background left her emotionally, psychologically, and socially incapable of handling that level of stress. Action was required, however, not out of judgment, but compassion—a little like Jesus' interaction with the woman caught in adultery.

> *Straightening up, Jesus said to her, "Woman, where are they? Did no one condemn you?" She said, "No one, Lord." And Jesus said, "I do not condemn you, either. Go. From now on sin no more"* (John 8:10-11).

As new creations who still make decisions that fall short of God's glory, we know God does not count our transgressions against us, so neither should we count these transgressions against them.

> *Now all these things are from God, who reconciled us to Himself through Christ and gave us the ministry of reconciliation, namely, that God was in Christ reconciling the world to Himself, not counting their trespasses against them, and He has committed to us the word of reconciliation* (2 Corinthians 5:18-19).

When we are the offended party—that is, the recipient of another's poor choices—our focus is to forgive. To discover how we can become more like Jesus in moments of distress.

> *You have heard that it was said, "You shall love your neighbor and hate your enemy." But I say to you, love your enemies and pray for those who persecute you* (Matthew 5:43-44).

In passing judgment on another, we condemn ourselves.

> *Therefore you have no excuse, everyone of you who passes judgment, for in that which you judge another, you condemn yourself; for you who judge practice the same things* (Romans 2:1).

Where there are ethical differences between people in which there is no absolute right or wrong, everyone is called to focus on their own relationship with God, being concerned with their own faith walk.

> *Who are you to judge the servant of another? To his own master he stands or falls; and he will stand, for the Lord is able to make him stand* (Romans 14:4).
>
> *But you, why do you judge your brother? Or you again, why do you regard your brother with contempt? For we will all stand before the judgment seat of God* (Romans 14:10).
>
> *So then each one of us will give an account of himself to God. Therefore let us not judge one another anymore, but rather determine this—not to put an obstacle or a stumbling block in a brother's way* (Romans 14:12-13).
>
> *The faith which you have, have as your own conviction before God. Happy is he who does not condemn himself in what he approves. But he who doubts is condemned if he eats, because his eating is not from faith; and whatever is not from faith is sin* (Romans 14:22-23).

The greater commandment establishes a requirement for New Testament living and spirituality to center our lives on knowing God's love through experience and encounter, not just knowing intellectually. From this place of knowing, we are to offer others the unconditional love we have received. The observable outcome of this expression of love is that we gather the well-being and worth of every person into our hearts of compassion. In pursuing this lifestyle and spirituality, we are on guard against the pervasive tendency to judge others, as when we do, we scatter and separate ourselves from others. When this occurs, we cannot be the answer to Jesus' prayer. We undermine the work of the Spirit in bringing the world to see that the Father sent His Son to restore us to oneness with God.

Summary

Jesus rewrote the second of the two great commandments of the Old Testament and gave us the *greater commandment.*

New Testament spirituality is to be established on knowing how much Jesus loves us and loving others in the same way.

The Law is no longer to be used to describe and assess righteousness. It is not the *source* of righteousness, but it is forever the *course of rightness.*

The Gospel seen through Old Testament eyes is a *closed system* where rules create boundaries that provide evidence that you are in or out.

The Gospel seen through New Testament eyes is a *centered system* where grace and mercy empower us to live like Jesus as we progressively surrender to His love for us and others.

The Law of the Kingdom of God is the place of being *one* with God and man.

When making disciples, Jesus emphasized: "teach them to observe all that I commanded you."

- Note the significance of the word "I" in the context of "commanded you."
- It is a command: "to love one another, as I have loved you."
- The place and meaning of "observe" is "to guard from loss by keeping your eye upon."

We live a lifestyle centered around love, empowered by abiding, based in revelation about how Jesus loves us, and knowing how deeply we are loved.

Nothing is to compete with love, yet we so readily reach for judgment rather than love, mercy, and compassion.

Questions and Activity

1. What are the implications for the way you currently live if you were to decide to establish your spirituality on the greater commandment of the New Testament?
2. Do you see the Gospel of the Kingdom through Old Testament or New Testament eyes?
3. What leads you to "take your eye off" how much you are loved by God and therefore impacts how you love others?
4. Did you take a Selah moment to consider whether you really grasp the truth that you are loved by God the Father in the same way, and to the same depth, that He loves Jesus?

Notes

1. Dallas Willard, *The Divine Conspiracy: Rediscovering Our Hidden Life in God* (New York, NY: HarperOne, 1997), 142.
2. Ibid., 160-161.
3. Boyd, *Repenting of Religion*, 48.

Chapter Three

THE GREAT PURSUIT

...Living in the Truth of Who We Really Are

My love of music and poetry spans a diverse range of genres. I find the band Coldplay fascinating and intriguing, particularly regarding the topics they address in their music.

Their album *Viva La Vida* and its signature song, meaning "long live life" or "the life lives," is always played very loudly in my car! The lyrics intrigued me, and some digging unearthed the following from the internet:

> Q magazine asked Chris Martin about the lyric on this song "I know Saint Peter won't call my name." The Coldplay lead singer replied: "It's about…You're not on the list. I was a naughty boy. It's always fascinated me that idea of finishing your life and then being analyzed on it. And it's that runs through most religions. That's why people blow up buildings. Because they think they're going to get lots of virgins. I always feel like saying, just join a band (cackles head off). That is the most frightening thing you could possibly say to somebody. Eternal damnation. I know this stuff because I studied it. I was into it all. I know it. It's still mildly terrifying to me. And this is serious."[1]

Chris' reply, "I know about this stuff because I studied it," reveals so much. The unfortunate reality is that the majority of people understand Christian spirituality through a predominantly Old Testament lens that cultural Christianity[2] has masterfully propagated. Such a view compromises Paul's revelatory insights into what it means to be a new creation and the mystery that Christ dwells in us.

To illustrate this, allow me to explore with you what you think happened when you put your trust in Jesus after you were born again.

Our journey to faith saw us, at some point, a distance away from a relationship with God. For some, we were further away than others. Then events began to take place that stimulated a process where we were asked to make a decision to put our trust in Jesus. We concluded that we wanted to live a life of following Jesus.

I have discovered that what most Christians believe occurred at the point of beginning a relationship with Jesus looks like this:

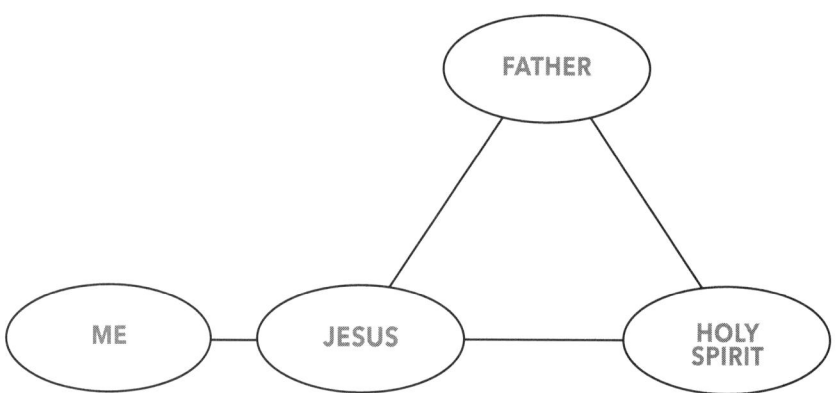

As followers of Jesus, we start attending church, where for the most part the underlying, and at times an explicit, message is that we are sinners saved by grace. The emphasis remains on sin and the call to change behavior to reflect the standards that God expects of us. The overarching impression is that God relates to me based on my behavior. Jesus is my friend who helps protect me from a Father prone to getting angry. I'm not sure how to relate to the Holy Spirit as He is the more intangible, ethereal one.

The net result is that we are left with the idea that there is a "brownie point system" at play around God's view of us. This is totally familiar to us based on how people express love to us. That is, I am liked, valued, and favored when I do what is expected. Conversely, from my childhood I have learned that when I do what is wrong, value and favor are withdrawn from me. Experiences such as these can remind us of the God of the Old Testament. Sometimes I feel close and accepted; other times, I feel distant and uncertain.

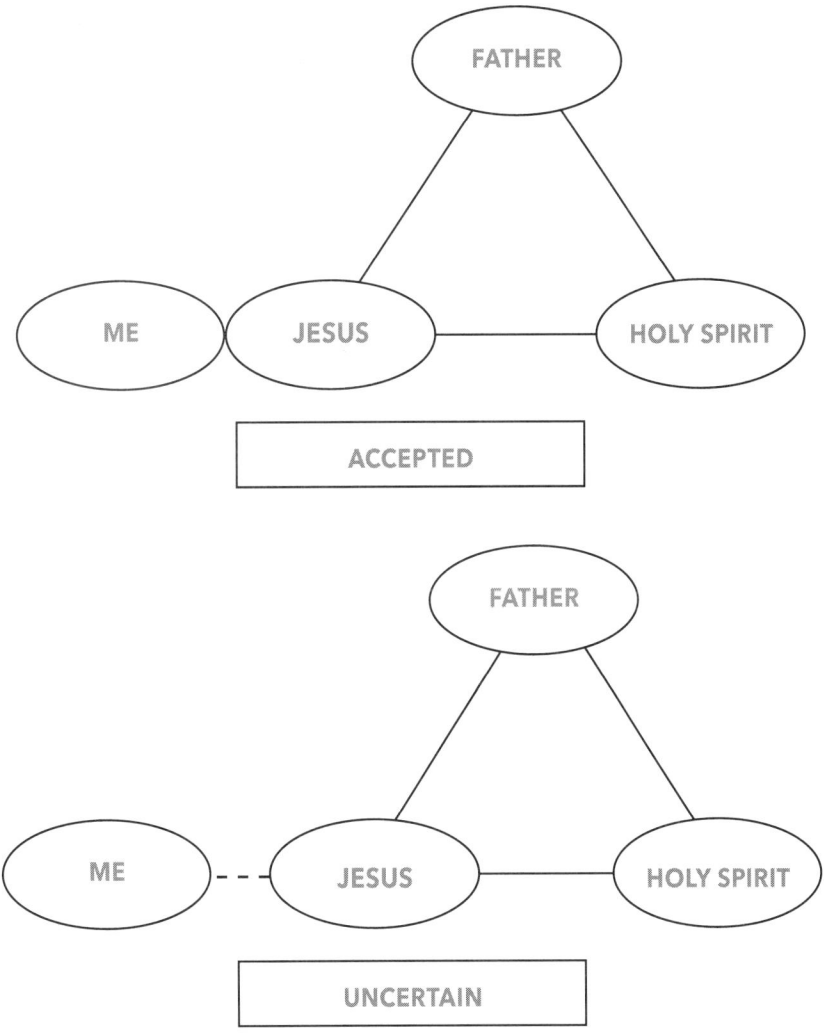

With this mind-set, my relationship with Jesus becomes performance and behavior management based. As such, it focuses me on my sin or good works as the defining point for how Jesus relates to me. I try harder to do what I am told is expected. I wonder how Jesus really loves me. When I think He loves me by assessing the appropriateness of my behavior, I relate to others in the same way. This results in a distorted expression of "love one another as I have loved you." Judgment is validated, even necessary and required, because a life of following Jesus is rule-based.

This proposition is supported by the Barna research group in their 2009 findings of religious views in America when they state:

> An overwhelming majority of self-identified Christians (81%) contend that spiritual maturity is achieved by following the rules in the Bible.[3]

Equally, it also reports that:

> Those pastors who made any attempt to measure maturity were more likely to gauge depth on the basis of participation in programs than to evaluate people's spiritual understanding or any type of transformational fruit in their lives.[4]

This explains their further assertion that:

> Millions of Americans have less trouble embracing Christ than they have embracing Christianity, but many people assume it is a package deal: that is, you cannot be a Christian without adopting the institutional framework and limitations of the Christian world. Young adults, in particular, find that unappealing.
>
> …Ultimately, in a culture where people are busy, distracted, confused and trying to keep it all together, there

is less loyalty to a faith brand than to self. The purpose of faith, for most Americans, is not so much to discover truth or to relate to a loving, praiseworthy deity as it is to become happy, successful, comfortable and secure. For a growing percentage of citizens, their sense of spirituality, more than Christianity, facilitates those outcomes.[5]

Spirituality and Christianity have been unnecessarily and dangerously separated by a focus on behavior and following the rules. This focus has been enhanced by a "closed set" understanding of Kingdom living. That is, Kingdom living is defined by a set of rules that God requires we follow to remain righteous and in good standing with Him. The way into a relationship with God and Kingdom living is through a prescribed way. All of which reinforces a performance base to our experience of receiving and giving love.

The good news of the Gospel of the Kingdom is the above *does not* represent what happened when we put our trust in Jesus and were born again. In contrast to the above, here is the reality of what occurred:

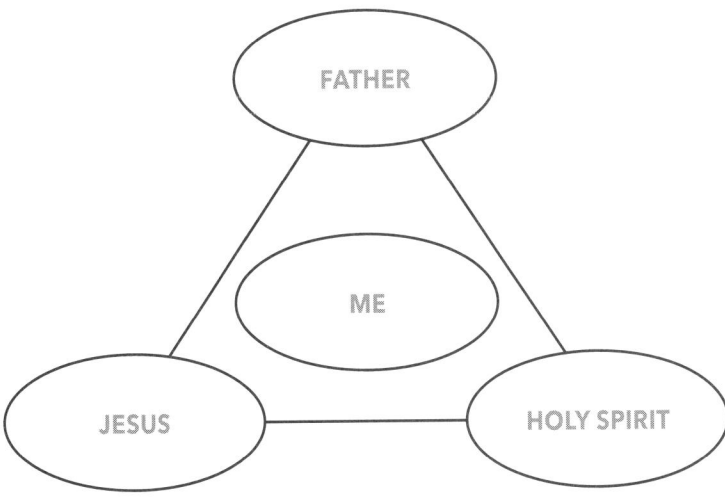

That is:

> *But when the fullness of the time came, God sent forth His Son, born of a woman, born under the Law, so that He might redeem those who were under the Law, that we might receive the adoption as sons. Because you are sons, God has sent forth the Spirit of His Son into our hearts, crying, "Abba! Father!" Therefore you are no longer a slave, but a son; and if a son, then an heir through God* (Galatians 4:4-7).

We have been redeemed (purchased the freedom of, saved, rescued, reclaimed, delivered from sin, and damnation) into a life of being a son/child of God. We are no longer slaves to a relationship with God based on performance and behavior management. We have been freed to inhabit a place of acceptance where all our sins have been forgiven.

> *Blessed be the God and Father of our Lord Jesus Christ, who has blessed us with every spiritual blessing in the heavenly places in Christ, just as He chose us in Him before the foundation of the world, that we would be holy and blameless before Him. In love He predestined us to adoption as sons through Jesus Christ to Himself, according to the kind intention of His will, to the praise of the glory of His grace, which He freely bestowed on us in the Beloved. In Him we have redemption through His blood, the forgiveness of our trespasses, according to the riches of His grace which He lavished on us* (Ephesians 1:3-8).

So, as a much-loved child of God, you:

- have received *every* spiritual blessing—you are complete;
- have been chosen—you are wanted on purpose;

- are holy and blameless—you are righteous in God's eyes;
- are adopted through Jesus to Himself—a new creation;
- have the forgiveness of all your trespasses—not focused on sin.

Your life as a follower of Jesus is to be characterized by belief management. That is, do you really, genuinely believe the attributes in the above list are what you have received, who you are, and how God sees you?

This truth stands in contrast to the previously described "closed set" and can be represented by the "centered set."

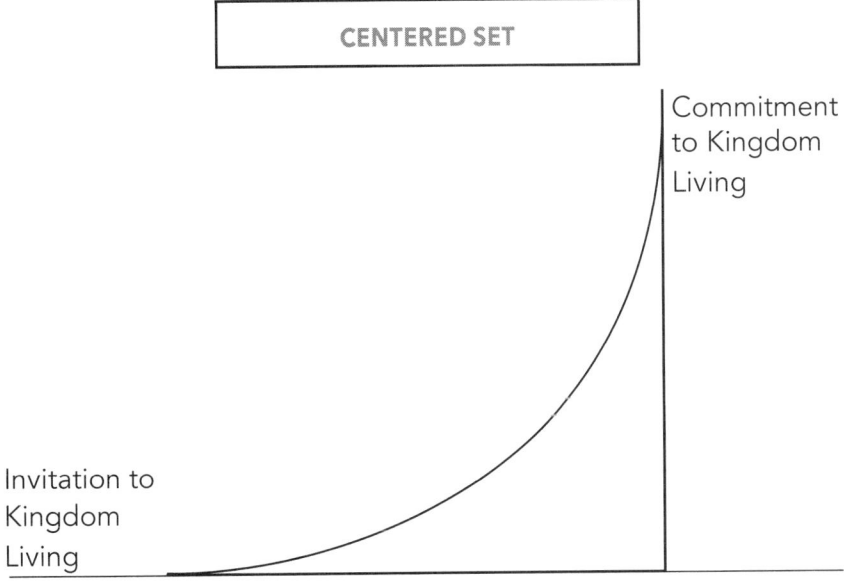

That is, Kingdom living and relationship with God are defined by a journey of discovery, including who we are in Christ. It is all invitational and begins with Jesus asking us to "come follow Me." It is a journey of surrender to His love and Lordship as we grow in our heart knowledge of being chosen, made holy, and being the beloved of God. Our spiritual maturity is measured by our transformation resulting in our growing commitment to live more and more like the one who loves us most deeply—Jesus.

The Power Adoption

Culturally, at the time of Jesus and Paul, one particular form of adoption was available to wealthy and powerful men who had no natural heir to pass on their inheritance to. They would consider all the adult males in their community and choose one whom they knew, had a history with, and were happy to pass on their inheritance to. Interestingly, it was not uncommon for natural children to be abandoned and receive no inheritance. Still, it was unlawful for adopted children to be abandoned.

To adopt an adult child, the person of power, wealth, and influence had to gain the permission of the birth parents. When the adoption was complete, the one adopted changed their name to that of the new "parents." They moved into a new home and carried new responsibilities, with new authority, representing another family's interests. Those who heard Paul's teaching that we are adopted children of God understood how being chosen by God represented being called by name. It meant belonging in a family with another father, with a place in the father's heart (and a mansion in heaven), responsible for representing Jesus well and carrying all authority in heaven and earth to represent the Kingdom of God. Equally, they had tangible examples that nothing can separate you from the love of God because of the legal position held by those who had been adopted.

Let's keep thinking this through.

Do you think Jesus was a servant of the world on behalf of the Father; or was Jesus a servant of the Father on behalf of the world?

If Jesus were a servant of the world, then human needs, including our needs, set the agenda, including my need as a sinner saved by grace to behave better. Need then forms the substance of my prayer life, where I am always looking for solutions and asking God to intervene. I am asking God to join Himself to what I need and am doing.

However, Jesus was a servant of the Father, and so are we. Consequently, my life, like Jesus' life, is focused on a relationship where I know He wants to say and show things to me. As such, I live a life of devotion, adoration, and love for God, where I am motivated to know God and be known by Him. I am asking God for His heart so that I can join myself to what is important to Him.

What I am advocating here is your consideration on how you view your relationship with God. What lens do you look through as you walk with God? Do you need to change the lens you are looking through to enhance and step into the fullness of all God has made available?

Peter had a lens resetting moment in Acts 10 when he had an open vision. He saw a white sheet appear with animals that, as a Jew, he was prohibited from eating. Three times Peter objected to being told he could eat what was on the sheet. The vision was to prepare Peter to understand that a new day had dawned in the Kingdom of God, where Gentiles were to be fully welcomed and embraced as the people of God. The thinking generated by an Old Testament reference point had to change to accommodate what God had done in Jesus.

Unfortunately, across the Body of Christ, there is more thinking from an Old Testament reference point than most of God's people realize. This hinders and, at times, prohibits followers of Jesus from fully pursuing the incredible inheritance God has granted us in Jesus.

Let's examine three Old Testament reference points that make it so difficult for us to believe what has taken place through Jesus.

Sin Consciousness

The first Old Testament reference point is that of sin consciousness, which for Paul is at odds with and battles against being conscious of our new-found adoption—*son consciousness.*

Romans 3:20 is our starting point:

> *Because by the works of the Law no flesh will be justified in His sight; for through the Law comes the knowledge of sin.*

The Old Testament framework for a relationship with God was adherence to the Law. By following the Law with good behavior management and offering sacrifices for forgiveness, Jews were confident that God would be well pleased with them. God would bless them and welcome them in the afterlife. These are the ideals of the cultural Christianity in which I was raised—as expressed through many denominations and epitomized in the endless media and literary characterizations of God who is upset with the sin of mankind. The belief is "as God is sin conscious, so we should be too."

As discussed previously, our natural motivations and inclinations to belong, be secure, and be significant are often satisfied by "right" behavior to gain acceptance. Cultures all around the world express love and receive love based on judgments around what is appropriate behavior worthy of love or, alternatively, punishment. Consequently, we live and are raised in cultures that focus us on good and bad behavior. That is a form and variation of sin consciousness.

However, as also discussed previously, sin is less about "right and wrong" based on a set of religious ideologies. It is more about being in right relationship with God, others, ourselves, and creation. Sinning involves attitudes and behaviors that create division in relationships and is a barrier to flourishing and whole relationships. Equally, righteousness can be tied to the fulfilment of the relationship between two persons more than to the fulfilment of a legalistic code—that is, remaining loyal to the demands of the relationship. So, when we read Paul's description of the place of the power of sin, he appears to be leading us away from approaching the topic of sin as "behavior management."

Hence, Paul is arguing that the works of the Law, used for attaining right standing with God, actually engender an awareness or preoccupation with behavior as sin. In Romans 3:23, Paul acknowledges that all have sinned and fall short of God's glory. However, his purpose here is not to highlight sin but to highlight the answer to sin:

> *But now apart from the Law the righteousness of God has been manifested, being witnessed by the Law and the Prophets, even the righteousness of God through faith in Jesus Christ for all those who believe; for there is no distinction* (Romans 3:21-22).

This is reinforced by Paul shortly after when he writes:

> *Even so consider yourselves to be dead to sin, but alive to God in Christ Jesus* (Romans 6:11).

Paul is calling us away from being sin conscious to becoming conscious of our new life and identity in Christ:

> *Being justified as a gift by His grace through the redemption which is in Christ Jesus* (Romans 3:24).

Paul explores this tension between sin consciousness and son consciousness further when he writes:

> *For I know that nothing good dwells in me, that is, in my flesh; for the willing is present in me, but the doing of the good is not. For the good that I want, I do not do, but I practice the very evil that I do not want. But if I am doing the very thing I do not want, I am no longer the one doing it, but sin which*

> *dwells in me. I find then the principle that evil is present in me, the one who wants to do good. For I joyfully concur with the law of God in the inner man, but I see a different law in the members of my body, waging war against the law of my mind and making me a prisoner of the law of sin which is in my members. Wretched man that I am! Who will set me free from the body of this death? Thanks be to God through Jesus Christ our Lord! So then, on the one hand I myself with my mind am serving the law of God, but on the other, with my flesh the law of sin* (Romans 7:18-25).
>
> *Therefore there is now no condemnation for those who are in Christ Jesus. For the law of the Spirit of life in Christ Jesus has set you free from the law of sin and of death* (Romans 8:1-2).

Paul powerfully asserts that his response to his sin is not to live with condemnation. Paul responds to his sin by relying on the Spirit of life in Christ Jesus to set him free from the law of sin and death. That is, he focuses on being conscious of his new identity as a son and relies on that identity to shape and form his life as a follower of Jesus. As we stay focused on our standing as sons of God, we can be led by the Spirit.

As we live as sons of God, we can be like Jesus because we begin to live as "heirs of God and fellow heirs with Christ." Being like Jesus is always undermined and stolen from us when we become sin conscious. When we are sin conscious, we are defined by, focused on, ruled by, and dictated to by our sense of being unworthy because of sin. When we are sin conscious, we come again under a spirit of slavery, leading to fear (see Rom. 8:15).

It is absolutely essential to recognize that our sin does not disqualify us from being sons of God. The story of the prodigal son in Luke 15 will help us at this point.

"I will get up and go to my father, and will say to him, 'Father, I have sinned against heaven, and in your sight; I am no longer worthy to be called your son; make me as one of your hired men.'" So he got up and came to his father. But while he was still a long way off, his father saw him and felt compassion for him, and ran and embraced him and kissed him. And the son said to him, "Father, I have sinned against heaven and in your sight; I am no longer worthy to be called your son." But the father said to his slaves, "Quickly bring out the best robe and put it on him, and put a ring on his hand and sandals on his feet; and bring the fattened calf, kill it, and let us eat and celebrate; For this son of mine was dead and has come to life again; he was lost and has been found." And they began to celebrate.

Now his older son was in the field, and when he came and approached the house, he heard music and dancing. And he summoned one of the servants and began inquiring what these things could be. And he said to him, "Your brother has come, and your father has killed the fattened calf because he has received him back safe and sound." But he became angry and was not willing to go in; and his father came out and began pleading with him. But he answered and said to his father, "Look! For so many years I have been serving you and I have never neglected a command of yours; and yet you have never given me a young goat, so that I might celebrate with my friends; but when this son of yours came, who has devoured your wealth with prostitutes, you killed the fattened calf for him." And he said to him, "Son, you have always been with me, and all that is mine is yours. But we had to celebrate and rejoice, for this brother of yours was dead and has begun to live, and was lost and has been found" (Luke 15:18-32).

The prodigal son was sin conscious to the point of believing he was not worthy of being his father's son. Worthiness was not a consideration for his father; he was not focused on his younger son's sin but only on his sonship. The father sought to restore him to that position, refusing to count the son's transgressions against him (unlike his older brother). The younger son, in the father's eyes, was never disqualified by his sin from being his son. In just such a way, God the Father does not negate, diminish, or lessen our right to be sons of God because of sin (see John 1:12). The devil, through religion and a works-based faith, is determined to stop us living as sons of God by leading us to be sin conscious. We live as sons of God by relying on the spirit of adoption, the spirit of life in Christ Jesus. and crying out "Abba! Father" even though we do sin.

Sin consciousness is the most destructive force that stops God's people living the abundant and lavish Christian life Jesus offers and being like Jesus in every way. Sin consciousness is unintentionally and inadvertently fueled by the performance bias of our national and ethnic cultures. Christians carry this bias into their faith life, and it is translated into works. "What must I do to stay saved and go to heaven?" In some respects, we are no better than our forefathers when we read:

> *I am amazed that you are so quickly deserting Him who called you by the grace of Christ, for a different gospel; which is really not another; only there are some who are disturbing you and want to distort the gospel of Christ. But even if we, or an angel from heaven, should preach to you a gospel contrary to what we have preached to you, he is to be accursed! As we have said before, so I say again now, if any man is preaching to you a gospel contrary to what you received, he is to be accursed!* (Galatians 1:6-9)

> *You foolish Galatians, who has bewitched you, before whose eyes Jesus Christ was publicly portrayed as crucified? This is the only thing I want to find out from you: did you receive the Spirit by the works of the Law, or by hearing with faith? Are you so foolish? Having begun by the Spirit, are you now being perfected by the flesh? Did you suffer so many things in vain—if indeed it was in vain? So then, does He who provides you with the Spirit and works miracles among you, do it by the works of the Law, or by hearing with faith?* (Galatians 3:1-5)

To stay focused on and conscious of our sonship, we need to defeat sin consciousness. To win this victory, we need to hear and understand what the Bible says about sin.

> *Namely, that God was in Christ reconciling the world to Himself, not counting their trespasses against them, and He has committed to us the word of reconciliation* (2 Corinthians 5:19).

As a result of Jesus' sacrifice on the cross, God is not counting *anyone's* trespass (sin) against them. There is no ledger in heaven where your sins are recorded. The imagined ledger of sinfulness does not need to be balanced through dedication, spiritual discipline, or commitment. This is an Old Testament concept that was changed through the work of the cross. The Kingdom of God is not a set of rules; it is a set of relationships. God is not looking to judge or condemn us; instead, He is focused on the restoration of the relationship. This truth is powerfully illustrated through the story of the woman caught in adultery (see John 8:1-11).

Relationships are not restored through threats of punishment. Hard to believe and accept? Let's keep looking.

> *When you were dead in your transgressions and the uncircumcision of your flesh, He made you alive together with Him, having forgiven us all our transgressions* (Colossians 2:13).

God has forgiven *all* your transgressions—past, present, and future. The blood of Jesus was sufficient to forgive you, and this is why anyone's sin—believer or prebeliever—is not counted against them. Your shame, guilt, and self-condemnation are not necessary. Shame and fear entered the heart of man because of sin (see Gen. 3:1-13). Yet Jesus despised the shame of the cross (see Heb. 12:2) and died naked so that we no longer have to live under the tyranny of shame, guilt, and condemnation.

This is truly good news! Too good for some. But wait, there's more!

> *Every priest stands daily ministering and offering time after time the same sacrifices, which can never take away sins; but He, having offered one sacrifice for sins for all time, sat down at the right hand of God, waiting from that time onward until His enemies be made a footstool for His feet. For by one offering He has perfected for all time those who are sanctified* (Hebrews 10:11-14).

One sacrifice for sins for all time has perfected those who are sanctified. Amazingly, your standing in the sight of God after you are born again is that of a perfect son. An heir of Christ as He was the firstborn among many brethren. This is why Paul confidently testifies in Colossians 1:21-22:

> *And although you were formerly alienated and hostile in mind, engaged in evil deeds, yet He has now reconciled you in His fleshly body through death, in order to present you before Him holy and blameless and beyond reproach.*

If you are a follower of Jesus, God sees you as holy, blameless, and beyond reproach. This is who you really are. Ephesians 1:3-7 affirms this position and relates it to being adopted as sons:

> *Blessed be the God and Father of our Lord Jesus Christ, who has blessed us with every spiritual blessing in the heavenly places in Christ, just as He chose us in Him before the foundation of the world, that we would be holy and blameless before Him. In love He predestined us to adoption as sons through Jesus Christ to Himself, according to the kind intention of His will, to the praise of the glory of His grace, which He freely bestowed on us in the Beloved. In Him we have redemption through His blood, the forgiveness of our trespasses, according to the riches of His grace.*

This is why you can approach the throne of grace with confidence (see Heb. 4:16). You are a son of God, and so you can learn to be like Jesus. This extraordinary good news is a mystery.

> *That is, the mystery which has been hidden from the past ages and generations, but has now been manifested to His saints, to whom God willed to make known what is the riches of the glory of this mystery among the Gentiles, which is Christ in you, the hope of glory* (Colossians 1:26-27).

We are one with Jesus.

> *I have been crucified with Christ; and it is no longer I who live, but Christ lives in me; and the life which I now live in the flesh I live by faith in the Son of God, who loved me and gave Himself up for me* (Galatians 2:20).

How is this possible? It is possible because of the cross of Jesus Christ.

> *So then as through one transgression there resulted condemnation to all men, even so through one act of righteousness there resulted justification of life to all men* (Romans 5:18).
>
> *Being justified as a gift by His grace through the redemption which is in Christ Jesus; whom God displayed publicly as a propitiation in His blood through faith. This was to demonstrate His righteousness, because in the forbearance of God He passed over the sins previously committed; for the demonstration, I say, of His righteousness at the present time, so that He would be just and the justifier of the one who has faith in Jesus* (Romans 3:24-26).

God has passed over the sins previously committed. This act of reconciliation, justification, and redemption was echoed in the Book of Exodus (chapter 12) when the angel of death passed over the houses whose doors were covered in the blood of a lamb. In this context, Paul writes:

> *Blessed is the man whose sin the Lord will not take into account* (Romans 4:8).

There remains a good and appropriate question of what are we to do about our sin? Clearly, we are not to be sin conscious.

> *Even so consider yourselves to be dead to sin, but alive to God in Christ Jesus* (Romans 6:11).

Yet it is equally clear that we can't just carry on sinning without some response.

> *What shall we say then? Are we to continue in sin so that grace may increase? May it never be! How shall we who died to sin still live in it?* (Romans 6:1-2)
>
> *And He, when He comes, will convict the world concerning sin and righteousness and judgment; concerning sin,*

because they do not believe in Me; and concerning righteousness, because I go to the Father and you no longer see Me; and concerning judgment, because the ruler of this world has been judged (John 16:8-11).

The Holy Spirit convicts of sin *"because they do not believe in Me."* I believe the sin that the Holy Spirit convicts people of is that of *unbelief*. This is the sin that separates a person from a relationship with the Father. I am unable to find any sense in the thought that the Holy Spirit convicts us of something that God is not taking into account. He has forgiven us and offered a sacrifice once and for all—that is, our transgressions and sin. The Father has punished and judged Jesus for all our sins. God placed all of our sins on Jesus and placed all of Jesus' righteousness on us (see 2 Cor. 5:21). Jesus identified with us at our worst so that we could be identified with Him at His best. We are righteous before God because of Jesus' actions and obedience on our behalf. This is the gift that He offers to all mankind. The gift already exists because of the death and resurrection of Jesus. Now the Father, through the Holy Spirit, is offering the opportunity to receive the gift. His offer comes with a conviction of unbelief because faith is necessary to receive it (see Rom. 3:26).

Once the sin of unbelief is dealt with and we are reconciled to God, the Holy Spirit convicts of *"righteousness, because I go to the Father and you no longer see Me"* (John 16:10). Jesus is pointing to the resurrection side of the cross. Before the cross, God judged and punished sin. At the cross, He judged and punished Jesus for all sin for all time. The issue of sin and its place in a person's life is changed dramatically when a person believes in Jesus as Lord and Savior. Now on the resurrection side of the cross, the Father is calling His people to righteousness. God does not call His people out on their sin, He calls them *up* into who they already are.

Similarly, the father of the prodigal son did not focus on the son's thought that his behavior was not worthy. The father responded by restoring him to his actual position of being his son. God is not interested in what is wrong; He is interested in what is *missing*. The Father is not disillusioned with us, as He never had any illusions about us in the first place. In the process of calling us up, the Holy Spirit will contrast the roots of the old nature that need to be removed with the person we already are in Jesus. However, at these times He is offering us freedom, not judgment. Again, this is why Paul calls us to be dead to sin and alive to God (see Rom. 6:11). It is *what* we believe, much more than how we behave, that is crucial.

A consequence of eating from the tree of knowledge of good and evil is to focus on behavior—both our own and others'. A focus on our own behavior often results in sin consciousness, which is then reinforced by Old Testament theology and the spirit of law and death. The net result is that we process our life with God by improving our behavior and stopping sin.

When we accept Jesus and agree with what the cross accomplished, we act from the tree of life (see John 14:6). What we believe about the cross connects us to the spirit of life and the New Testament emphasis on relationship (see Matt. 22:36-40). The net result is that we are free to focus our life with God through our relationship as a son and how our beliefs impact our relationship with the Father.

The awareness of our sin presents a learning opportunity to be more like Jesus. The Spirit is saying you can move from there to here and in so doing be more like Jesus. We are being transformed into the same image from glory to glory, just as from the Lord, the Spirit (see 2 Cor. 3:18). Most importantly, the awareness of sin should never be entertained as a reason to be disqualified from living as a son.

> *The gift is not like that which came through the one who sinned; for on the one hand the judgment arose from one*

transgression resulting in condemnation, but on the other hand the free gift arose from many transgressions resulting in justification. For if by the transgression of the one, death reigned through the one, much more those who receive the abundance of grace and of the gift of righteousness will reign in life through the One, Jesus Christ (Romans 5:16-17).

The Holy Spirit convicts us of righteousness as it is this free gift that leads us into a knowledge of the Father.

More than that, I count all things to be loss in view of the surpassing value of knowing Christ Jesus my Lord, for whom I have suffered the loss of all things, and count them but rubbish so that I may gain Christ, and may be found in Him, not having a righteousness of my own derived from the Law, but that which is through faith in Christ, the righteousness which comes from God on the basis of faith, that I may know Him and the power of His resurrection and the fellowship of His sufferings, being conformed to His death; in order that I may attain to the resurrection from the dead (Philippians 3:8-11).

Understanding righteousness changes the way we view ourselves, and this, in turn, affects how we engage with our life and spirituality. Somehow King David was able to see things beyond his own time, and this is illustrated from Psalm 23:3:

He restores my soul;
He guides me in the paths of righteousness
For His name's sake.

The Holy Spirit wants to show us how righteous we are.

But seek first His kingdom and His righteousness, and all these things will be added to you (Matthew 6:33).

Put another way, know and understand His Kingdom and His righteousness and all these things will be added to you. Very few Christians have a heart-felt understanding of His righteousness and what it means for them. Without that understanding, there will be limitations and restrictions in their experience as disciples of Jesus. Paul writes:

> *For the kingdom of God is not eating and drinking, but righteousness and peace and joy in the Holy Spirit* (Romans 14:17).

We can eat and drink to sustain our bodies to physically interact with life and all it brings. We need to sustain our spiritual lives to fully undertake the assignments we have been given to see the Kingdom of God advanced. This involves partaking of the qualities that righteousness, peace, and joy bring to us. The free gift of righteousness helps me to reign in life, adds to my fruitfulness in God's Kingdom, and positions me to live as a much-loved son of God and heir with Christ (see Rom. 5:17; 7:4; 8:10-17).

Fred Faller, in his insightful article "Right or Righteous" states:

> What do you think of when you hear the word "righteousness"? About a year ago I was challenged about my understanding of the nature of righteousness in the Bible and in my daily living. J.P. Tynes introduced the idea in a class that the word used for "righteousness" in the Old Testament carries a deeply embedded cultural concept. The challenge was that this concept was more tied to the fulfillment of the relationship between two persons than to the fulfillment of a legalistic code. Thinking like an Old Testament Jew, even two thieves could be considered "righteous" in their relationship to one another if it

were characterized by sharing, fairness, camaraderie and loyalty.[6]

Also in James 5:16 we find:

The effective prayer of a righteous man can accomplish much.

If I approach God's throne of grace with the certainty of my righteousness due to the finished work of the cross, my prayers can change natural realities. Just as Jesus changed natural realities, so can I.

I love Eugene Peterson's translation in *The Message* of First John 3:18-22:

My dear children, let's not just talk about love; let's practice real love. This is the only way we'll know we're living truly, living in God's reality. It's also the way to shut down debilitating self-criticism, even when there is something to it. For God is greater than our worried hearts and knows more about us than we do ourselves.

And friends, once that's taken care of and we're no longer accusing or condemning ourselves, we're bold and free before God! We're able to stretch our hands out and receive what we asked for because we're doing what he said, doing what pleases him.

Do not allow shame, guilt, and condemnation to rob you or your confidence before God and the knowledge that you have the standing of a son of God and an heir of Christ Jesus. The sin that inhabited our old nature has deep roots. It is a daily work of grace to conquer it. We need Jesus to be formed in us (see Gal. 4:19), but as an act of learning.

We are becoming everything we can be for Him at His pace and under the care of His coaches. Repentance is remorse for the way we have hurt the Lord. John 14:15 says, *"If you love Me, you will keep My commandments."*

A works-based paradigm hears this as, "If you love Me, you won't mess up or do anything wrong." A grace-based paradigm hears, "If you love Me, you won't do anything to hurt Me." So repentance in the Gospel of grace is saying sorry and being thankful for the forgiveness I already have and asking for insight to learn and keep walking.

In the Old Testament, the Lord used judgment to draw Israel's attention to their sin. Today Christians who reference Old Testament ways will interpret difficult times as God judging their sin. Yet Romans 5:1-2 says we have peace with God:

> *Therefore, having been justified by faith, we have peace with God through our Lord Jesus Christ, through whom also we have obtained our introduction by faith into this grace in which we stand; and we exult in hope of the glory of God.*

So, the Holy Spirit convicts prebelievers of unbelief because the Father longs to be reconciled to all men (see 2 Cor. 5:18-21). The Holy Spirit convicts believers of their righteousness so that they learn to walk in what the cross was for them. Then the Holy Spirit convicts believers concerning judgment because the ruler of this world, satan, has been judged. The Father wants believers to undertake life's battles from the position that *the victory has been won.*

Relationships with the Law

The way we relate to the law from the Old Testament is the second reference point that hinders us in fully pursuing the incredible inheritance God has granted us in Jesus.

The Old Testament has many helpful and pertinent things to say about God's best for us. Shalom, or the way God originally intended things to be, how to walk with God and wisdom, and God's nature and character. However, while God never changes, He did change the contract by which He relates to mankind. A line was drawn in the sand through Jesus' life, death, and resurrection so that things are now very different.

Paradigm of Acceptance Work *from* Love	Paradigm of Performance Work *for* Love
HIS BUSINESS: What is He saying and doing Faith and obedience Concern for signs and wonders Whose presence matters How do I get to enter God's world	**MY BUSINESS:** Being in control Avoiding fear Concern for reputation Who is present How do I get God to enter my world
WHAT'S FIRST FOR HIM: Being Obedience Vulnerable and weak Grace	**WHAT'S FIRST FOR ME:** Doing Being right Gifts and abilities Activity
MY FOCUS IS ON/I CARE ABOUT: His majesty His power His promises His life	**MY FOCUS IS ON/I CARE ABOUT:** Outcomes Opinions Self Safety
OUTCOMES: God's love defined by revelation Faith in nature and character of God	**OUTCOMES:** God's love defined by circumstances Sight is activated over faith

Here we need to revisit the truth that there has been a system change in the way the law is used to achieve righteousness with God that has made the old way obsolete. It has been totally set aside because it was weak and useless.

> *For when the priesthood is changed, of necessity there takes place a change of law also.*
>
> *…For, on the one hand, there is a setting aside of a former commandment because of its weakness and uselessness* (for the Law made nothing perfect), *and on the other hand there is a bringing in of a better hope, through which we draw near to God* (Hebrews 7:12, 18-19).
>
> *After saying above, "Sacrifices and offerings and whole burnt offerings and sacrifices for sin You have not desired, nor have You taken pleasure in them"* (which are offered according to the Law), *then He said, "Behold, I have come to do Your will." He takes away the first in order to establish the second. By this will we have been sanctified through the offering of the body of Jesus Christ once for all* (Hebrews 10:8-10).

The problem with the old way is that after showing us our sin, the law offers no real solutions.

> *Now we know that whatever the Law says, it speaks to those who are under the Law, so that every mouth may be closed and all the world may become accountable to God; because by the works of the Law no flesh will be justified in His sight; for through the Law comes the knowledge of sin* (Romans 3:19-20).
>
> *Why the Law then? It was added because of transgressions, having been ordained through angels by the agency of a mediator, until the seed would come to whom the promise had been made. Now a mediator is not for one party only; whereas God is only one. Is the Law then contrary to the promises of God? May it never be! For if a law had been given which was able to impart life, then righteousness would indeed have been based on law. But the Scripture has shut up everyone*

> *under sin, so that the promise by faith in Jesus Christ might be given to those who believe. But before faith came, we were kept in custody under the law, being shut up to the faith which was later to be revealed. Therefore the Law has become our tutor to lead us to Christ, so that we may be justified by faith* (Galatians 3:19-24).

Living by the law, or any rules and regulations, is an all or nothing proposition.

> *For as many as are of the works of the Law are under a curse; for it is written, "Cursed is everyone who does not abide by all things written in the book of the law, to perform them"* (Galatians 3:10).
>
> *For whoever keeps the whole law and yet stumbles in one point, he has become guilty of all* (James 2:10).
>
> *Therefore, my brethren, you also were made to die to the Law through the body of Christ, so that you might be joined to another, to Him who was raised from the dead, in order that we might bear fruit for God* (Romans 7:4).

For Paul, this also included using the Ten Commandments to measure and assess our relationship with God. When they are used this way, they minister death, bring condemnation, and represent a fading glory.

> *But if the ministry of death, in letters engraved on stones, came with glory, so that the sons of Israel could not look intently at the face of Moses because of the glory of his face, fading as it was, how will the ministry of the Spirit fail to be even more with glory? For if the ministry of condemnation has glory, much more does the ministry of righteousness abound in glory. For indeed what had glory, in this case has no glory because of the glory that surpasses it. For if that which fades away*

was with glory, much more that which remains is in glory (2 Corinthians 3:7-11).

Previously, I established that the law has not been done away with; it is the use of the law that is significant. The law does have a specific purpose for one particular group of people.

> *For God has not given us a spirit of timidity, but of power and love and discipline. Therefore do not be ashamed of the testimony of our Lord or of me His prisoner, but join with me in suffering for the gospel according to the power of God, who has saved us and called us with a holy calling, not according to our works, but according to His own purpose and grace which was granted us in Christ Jesus from all eternity* (2 Timothy 1:7-9).

> *But before faith came, we were kept in custody under the law, being shut up to the faith which was later to be revealed. Therefore the Law has become our tutor to lead us to Christ, so that we may be justified by faith. But now that faith has come, we are no longer under a tutor* (Galatians 3:23-25).

Many of God's people seem to see who Jesus is for their salvation and the law is to guide their relationship with God. This is not supported by Scripture as evidenced by the following.

I am dead to the law.

> *Therefore, my brethren, you also were made to die to the Law through the body of Christ, so that you might be joined to another, to Him who was raised from the dead, in order that we might bear fruit for God* (Romans 7:4).

> *For through the Law I died to the Law, so that I might live to God* (Galatians 2:19).

I'm not under the law.

> *For sin shall not be master over you, for you are not under law but under grace* (Romans 6:14).

I am free from the law.

> *For he who has died is freed from sin* (Romans 6:7).

I am not supervised by the law.

> *But now that faith has come, we are no longer under a tutor* (Galatians 3:25).

Christ is the end of the law for me.

> *For Christ is the end of the law for righteousness to everyone who believes* (Romans 10:4).

As a follower of Jesus, my relationship with God is not defined by my behavior. I am not walking with God based on behavior or a set of rules to act as a compass, guide, or help toward spiritual growth. We are called to discover a personal relationship with God based on unconditional love, resulting in acceptance and the opportunity in the newness of being adopted and the freedom that the Spirit leads us into.

> *For he who has died is freed from sin* (Romans 6:7).
> *But if you are led by the Spirit, you are not under the Law* (Galatians 5:18).
> *For you were called to freedom, brethren; only do not turn your freedom into an opportunity for the flesh, but through love serve one another* (Galatians 5:13).

N.T. Wright in *The Climax of the Covenant* summarizes this when he writes:

> The Torah (law of Moses at Sinai) is given for a specific period of time. And is then set aside—not because it was a bad thing now happily abolished, but because it was a good thing whose purpose had now been accomplished.[7]

Justification and Adoption

The third consequence of an Old Testament reference point that hinders us is the way both sin consciousness and our relationship to the law have focused Christian spirituality onto the New Testament theology of justification. This has been at the expense of moving into a full and vibrant embrace of the theology of adoption—that we are new creations.

A contributing factor is the historical preference for Augustinian theology of God's relationship with people over the theology of Athanasius.

Aurelius Augustine (364–430) is now known as Saint Augustine of Hippo. Augustine is one of the Latin Fathers of the church. He is widely recognized as perhaps the most significant Christian thinker after Paul. His distinct theological style shaped Latin Christianity, and later Roman and Protestant theology, in a way surpassed only by Scripture. Augustine represents the most influential adaptation of the ancient Platonic tradition of philosophy with Christian theology.

Athanasius of Alexandria (296–373) is also known as Athanasius the Confessor and Athanasius the Apostolic. Athanasius is labelled as the "Father of Orthodoxy" in the Eastern Orthodox Church. He was the first person to identify the same 27 books of the New Testament that are in use today. Athanasius' theology emerged through his defense against the heresy of Arius. Arius proposed that if the Father begat the Son, there was a time that the Son did not exist. Athanasius contended that such an idea denied the Trinity. Hence, Athanasius became known as the chief defender of Trinitarianism.

Augustinian theology is centered around two questions. What is God like? The answer—He is holy. What is man like? The answer—he is a sinner. These answers result in seeing God as a judge who views people as law breakers for whom a price had to be paid. This approach can be characterized as being a "Genesis Chapter 3 Model," where the focus is on the problem of sin.

Athanasian theology is centered around the question, "How do the Trinity relate to one another?" The answer is that they live in a covenant community of love where they respond with mutual honor for one another in cooperative relationship. This answer results in seeing God as a judge who is liberating oppressed people, putting things right, and protecting the integrity of His ways. This approach can be characterized as being a "Genesis Chapter 1 Model," where the focus is the joy of creation and relationship.

The emphasis of Augustinian theology comes down to judgment for wrongdoing. This is known as *propitiation*. That is, Jesus paid the penalty for the sin of mankind. When a person puts their trust in Jesus as Lord and Savior, they receive His righteousness and are now going to Heaven. Therefore, the death of Jesus was a sacrifice to satisfy God's judgment and avoid His wrath and the eternal desolation of hell.[8] This accurately represents the theology of justification and is rightly required for salvation.

The emphasis of Athanasian theology comes down to the removal of sin and its power. This is known as *expiation*. That is, Jesus died so that broken relationship is healed and fellowship with God is restored. When a person puts their trust in Jesus as Lord and Savior, He makes His home in them, thus bringing eternal quality of life in this world. Therefore, the death of Jesus was a sacrifice that benefited the recipient, changing their identity to that of children of God. This rightly represents the theology of adoption, which is required for us to be in the world as Jesus was in the world.

Augustine's status as the most influential Christian thinker after Paul has resulted in the theology of justification being over-emphasized at the expense of the theology of adoption. I view the theology of justification as the doorway into a mansion known as the theology of adoption. Justification based in propitiation is absolutely required for adoption based in expiation. However, we are not to camp in the doorway of justification; we are to walk through it to explore the inheritance associated with adoption. That is, who we are in Him and who He wants to be for us. This is why Paul emphasized adoption by using the thought and language of "Christ within you" over 160 times in his letters.

EMPHASIS ON JUSTIFICATION RESULTS IN:	EMPHASIS ON ADOPTION RESULTS IN:
A focus on managing behavior	A focus on identity and being a child of God
A spirituality focused on moral conformity	A spirituality focused on love
Being sin conscious	Being alive to the goodness and kindness of God
Judgment before mercy	Mercy where love reaches through any offence
Truth is a set of principles	Truth is a person
A relationship that is contractual in nature	A relationship that is covenantal in nature

I want to illustrate this point by considering that the theology of justification is founded on the truth that Jesus died and rose again *for* us. The theology of adoption moves further into the foundation that Jesus died *as* us, to do something to us and with us.

The first Adam's sin, as our federal representative, took the whole human race into sin. Hence, the death of Jesus as the second Adam was a federally represented death where we all died in Him to sin.

> *For the love of Christ controls us, having concluded this, that one died for all, therefore all died; and He died for all, so that they who live might no longer live for themselves, but for Him who died and rose again on their behalf* (2 Corinthians 5:14-15).

That *one died for all, therefore, all died* is the truth echoed in Romans 6:10-11:

> *For the death that He died, He died to sin once for all; but the life that He lives, He lives to God. Even so consider yourselves to be dead to sin, but alive to God in Christ Jesus.*

For the death He died, He died to sin once and for all. Jesus died *as* us so that when we put our trust in Him and are born again we become holy and blameless and all our sins—past, present, and future—are forgiven.

So, Jesus died *for us* so that we would receive forgiveness:

> *Peter said to them, "Repent, and each of you be baptized in the name of Jesus Christ for the forgiveness of your sins; and you will receive the gift of the Holy Spirit"* (Acts 2:38).

And Jesus died *as us* to do something *to us* and *with us* for His life to flow *through* us:

He who believes in Me, as the Scripture said, "From his innermost being will flow rivers of living water" (John 7:38).

Next, Jesus died *for us* so that we could live in God's reality, rule, and reign now:

For God so loved the world, that He gave His only begotten Son, that whoever believes in Him shall not perish, but have eternal life (John 3:16).

And Jesus died *as us* to do something *to us* and *with us* for God's reality, rule, and reign to invade earth through us:

Truly, truly, I say to you, he who believes in Me, the works that I do, he will do also; and greater works than these he will do; because I go to the Father (John 14:12).

Finally, Jesus died *for us* so that the problem of sin was dealt with:

You know that He appeared in order to take away sins; and in Him there is no sin (1 John 3:5).

And Jesus died *as us* to do something *to us* and *with us* for us to live as children of God:

Therefore if anyone is in Christ, he is a new creature; the old things passed away; behold, new things have come (2 Corinthians 5:17).

Adoption and Being a New Creation

Before exploring together how to live as an adopted child of God, we must jump into some more complex theology. We need to understand the difference between *"knowing this, that our old self was crucified with Him"* (Rom. 6:6), and *"you lay aside the old self...and put on the new self"*

(Eph. 4:22-24). In the simplest of terms, this can be seen as the relationship between truth and practice. That is, our new identity must result in thinking about ourselves in a new way, which in turn gives way to behaving differently, as behavior is always the echo of belief.

What is the entry point into understanding this relationship between the old man that is dead—so it can't be in process (see Rom. 6:6)—and the body of sin that is alive and actually in process (see Eph. 4:22). We begin by looking at Colossians 3:3: *"For you have died and your life is hidden with Christ in God."*

The context of this verse is Paul's exploration of God's mystery—that is, Christ Himself (see Col. 2:3). In contrast to the observation that they have been deluded by persuasive arguments and prevailing philosophies (see Col. 2:4,8), Paul continues by referring to the tradition of men and elementary principles of the world that, as we have previously established, create human cultures and spirituality based on following rules and regulations. This then results in mind-sets where our identity, value, and worth are found in our own efforts and measured through performance-based outcomes. The net result is the creation of an old man who died when we placed our trust in Jesus, and we now have a new life that is hidden with Christ in God. The old man and life we lived is dead and buried; the life we now live, we live by faith through who we are in Jesus. That is, the life we are now wired to live from, our inner man, is the life that Christ Himself lives.

This mystery is profound, so hang in with me as I find language to help us grasp the measure of it. Romans 6:5-7 declares:

> *For if we have become united with Him in the likeness of His death, certainly we shall also be in the likeness of His resurrection, knowing this, that our old self was crucified with Him, in order that our body of sin might be done away with, so that we would no longer be slaves to sin; for he who has died is freed from sin.*

As a result of my union with Christ, I have died with Him and the old self is buried with Him. Accepting that I have risen again with Him, then I am dead to sin as a realm that I live in and that can reign over my life. I have finished with it. It has nothing to do with me. And it is not my nature.

If my old man has been crucified and is dead and buried, then I can't be putting this off as it is already gone. So, when Paul talks of putting off or laying aside the old self in Ephesians 4:22 and Colossians 3:9, this must be something different.

Do not lie to one another, since you laid aside the old self with its evil practices.

As part of the wisdom for managing the mystery of Christ in our lives, Paul, in Colossians 3:3, declares the same truth in Romans 6:6—that our old man is dead. Yet a few verses later in Colossians he is stating that there is something called our old self that is laid aside and we are to put on the new self.

We must investigate—what is the old self or the flesh, as it is referred to in Galatians 4:16-24? Romans 7:22-23 gives us a clue.

For I joyfully concur with the law of God in the inner man, but I see a different law in the members of my body, waging war against the law of my mind and making me a prisoner of the law of sin which is in my members.

What if the members of the body are things like the mind, tongue, hunger, and sexual desire? These are recognizable as being used by my old man, my sin nature, for the purposes of sin. My mind is used to conceive of such things as anger, greed, and evil intent toward others. My tongue is used to gossip, express pride, blaspheme, and so on. My hunger to be a glutton and my sexual desires expressed in lustful behavior and pursuits—all have been affected by sin and have been governed by it.

What if the old self is the expression of sin through my instincts, motivations, propensities, and various urges and desires of my body? It is like physical muscle memory. When a movement is repeated over time, a long-term memory is created for that task, eventually allowing it to be performed with little to no conscious effort. Consequently, the old self can be viewed as the conversations, conduct, or behaviors that used to characterize the old man.

We put off the old self, no longer seeing ourselves as we once were. We see ourselves as we really are—new creations in Christ. We begin to want to put on new ways of behaving and being so that we are increasingly being conformed to the image of Jesus Christ. After all, behavior is always the echo of belief.

We are transformed through the joining together of the Word and Spirit when we learn to behold who we really are (see 2 Cor. 3:18). And, when we present ourselves in humility to God as living and holy sacrifices (see Rom. 12:1-2). This is how the world sees and experiences the reality of Jesus through us. Paul does not call us to behave a certain way to become something we are not. He invites us to know who we already are in Christ and to think and live accordingly.

How we do this is the subject of the next chapter.

Summary

Spirituality and Christianity have been unnecessarily and dangerously separated by a focus on behavior and following the rules.

Our spiritual maturity is measured by our transformation resulting in our growing commitment to live more and more like Jesus.

What we think about God is the most important thing in the world.

Old Testament thinking is strongly present in the church today and creates frameworks that make it difficult for us to believe what has taken place through Jesus.

Sin consciousness needs to be overcome through being conscious of our new life and identity in Christ.

Understanding righteousness changes the way we view ourselves and this, in turn, affects how we engage with our life and spirituality.

Many of God's people seem to see Jesus as for salvation and the law is to guide their relationship with God.

As a follower of Jesus, my relationship with God is not defined by my behavior.

We are to embrace the theology of justification as a springboard *into* the theology of adoption.

The relationship between the old self being crucified and laying aside the old self to put on the new self is one between truth and practice.

Questions and Activity

1. If you measure your spirituality by how well you follow the rules, what needs to change for you to measure it by transformation?
2. How would you design an approach to your spirituality that pursues, welcomes, and enhances change and transformation?
3. Name and describe three ways of thinking in your life that need to change to move from being sin conscious into being son conscious?
4. What does it mean *to* you and *for* you that you have been adopted by God into His family?

Notes

1. Chris Martin, qtd. in SongFacts, "Viva La Vida by Coldplay," accessed September 26, 2020, https://www.songfacts.com/facts/coldplay/viva-la-vida.

2. Cultural Christianity refers to an identification with Christian values and culture that has been significantly influenced by people's religious observance framed from a family background, personal experiences, and the social and cultural environment in which they were raised. These influences do not significantly rely on the knowledge of God brought by Jesus, Paul, and the writers of the New Testament. Rather, they draw on how church leaders throughout history have relied on the adherence to rules and regulations to control followers and defend the institution of church.
3. Barna Group, "Barna Studies the Research, Offers a Year-in-Review Perspective." https://www.barna.com/research/barna-studies-the-research-offers-a-year-in-review-perspective.
4. Ibid.
5. Ibid.
6. Fred Faller, "Right or Righteous," Disciples Today, October 03, 2017, https://www.disciplestoday.org/bible-study/digging-deeper/item-8714-right-or-righteous.
7. N.T. Wright, *The Climax of the Covenant: Christ and the Law in Pauline Theology* (Minneapolis, MN: T&T Clark, 1993), 181. I will explore in depth the consequences of this insight in *Radically Restored to Oneness with One Another*.
8. It should be noted that in the Gospels, there is no link between a penal death of Jesus and avoidance of God's wrath. Jesus' death in the Gospels is connected to forgiveness and an expression of love. The emphasis rests on the life that Jesus gives that enables a person to be free.

Chapter Four

THE GREAT LEARNING CURVE

...Living as a Much-Loved Child of God

ONE OF THE MANY PRIVILEGES OF MY LIFE IS TO HAVE FRIENDS WHO help me to see what I haven't seen and to know what has eluded me in my pursuit of knowledge. Graham Cooke is one such friend who has walked with me for over 20 years.

Graham's insights into living from the knowledge of who we already are in Christ so that we think and behave accordingly are profound, instructive, applicable, and life-giving. Graham has produced a remarkable teaching series, *"The Way God Walks with Us,"*[1] which is housed on his Brilliant TV channel and app. In the first episode of season one, "You're Accepted!" he brings the following prophetic word, as though God Himself was speaking to us. This captures the basis for how to yield to the truth of who we already are in Christ, to understand how God sees us, to know what life with God can really be like.

> Beloved,
> I welcome you, just as you are, into My whole heart. There's no condemnation, no judgment. I have no suspicions about you.

Acceptance is not you making yourself acceptable to Me, it begins with *Me* making acceptance freely available because Christ is in you. No other reason.

You cannot earn acceptance. You cannot acquire it by discipline. You cannot merit acceptance by your behavior. It is a relational gift from Me to you, earned by Jesus and acquired by His sacrifice.

His presence in you creates a place of acceptance and affection in My heart just as Jesus does. In the same way!

I start by coming to you with all the promises of what I will never do to you:

I will never leave you nor forsake you.

I will never lie to you.

I will never forget about you.

I will never leave you comfortless.

I will never run out of mercy.

I will never grow weary.

I will never fail to keep My promises

And I will never, ever change.

Those are absolutes for Me.

When you accept what Jesus has done to make you acceptable to Me, your trust will rise in line with our delight. When you agree that I have accepted you totally and completely in Jesus, peace will overtake you.

When the work is challenged by the enemy, by circumstances, and by your own weakness, you can find the place of acceptance by your agreement with Me.

Beloved, you will only be able to learn in an environment where you feel safe, loved, and accepted. When you open your heart to the truth that acceptance began with Me, not you, you'll feel safe and confident in your development.

You know what I love about that for you? It means that you can relax. You can be at peace in your learning. You can live with Me in the same delight that I have in your process of maturity!

You are accepted in the Beloved whilst walking through the process of learning to be Christ-like.

All your learning is covered in Me!

My Empowering presence of grace won't excuse you, but it also will never blame or shame you. The Holy Spirit will ask you instead, "What did you learn?" and "Who would you like to become because of that?"

That's what matters most to Me. I won't minimize your shortcomings, but I will ***totally*** accept you in the midst of them!

Repentance is My gift that allows you to learn, turn, and discover a better way of living with Me.

You're accepted in those times because the debt has been paid for where you're still being transformed into the image of Christ. You are debt-free in Him!

I can't hold anything against you because I already held all those things against Jesus on the cross. I held ***Him*** accountable for your deficits, and all the things you could ever be accused of have been nailed to His cross.

That's why We don't want you to judge yourself or others for what you're yet to learn. We're not judging you for it because the price for all your learning has been paid.

Beloved, your role is choosing your response to how We walk with you:

Old or new.

Flesh or spirit.

Religion or relationship.

Tradition or newness of life.

The way We walk with you can be the difference maker in all your life situations—so choose Us!

We know that you live in a world where Christian performance rules—where people wear masks to hide their perceived and real deficits. We watch people needlessly trying to be good enough for Us, fearing judgment and rejection. Self-righteousness, pride, and fear of dependence imprison our beloved ones.

When people feel insecure about their identity, they are subject to the fear that, "If you really knew me you would reject me." To feel safe, they believe they need to be in control, never showing vulnerability or need.

Beloved, that is a prison and lifestyle that Jesus came to set you free from.

Our acceptance is the master key that sets you free from performance. It breaks your bondages and makes it safe to remove the mask. The reality of Our acceptance takes the risk away and gives you the courage to say, "This is who I am and this is where I'm at right now."

It allows you to live every day in the humility and peace of transparency—to be free enough to laugh and humble enough to not hide from your God or acquiesce to the fear of man.

In humility, what other people think of you loses its power to rob you of your learning opportunities for fear of humiliation. That's the gift of walking with Us! We love mercy, so you can too!

You'll experience the delight of walking humbly with Us. You know who you are without Us—no need to hide it. But you also are confident in who you are *with* us! The person who truly knows that they are accepted in the Beloved lives in that freedom. That is *you*, Beloved!

You can live feeling the weight of mercy on your life. You can accept others right where they are because you have agreed with God and accept yourself where you are today.

Acceptance removes the need to prove your self-worth and enables you to live in your true relationship with Me—not your performance and good works. Jesus was the Perfect One. His gift of righteousness covers you while you're growing up into all things in Christ.

You're saved once, but you're being redeemed every day.

Being accepted in Jesus is a huge and powerful gift that is designed to overwhelm you with My love, kindness, mercy, and goodness. Let that overwhelm you.

This is your absolute Truth at this point. I already know everything about you—good, bad, or otherwise. All of your low places are taken into account as part of your learning process in Christ.

I know what I am upgrading and transforming in you. There is nothing that upsets Me because Jesus has already done the heavy lifting. Now We are working on your process of sanctification into Our image and likeness.

Think of it this way. The One who knows you best loves you the most.

Be vulnerable to our loving-kindness, grace, and mercy. Acceptance builds a bridge of trust in our relationship. It confidently spans the gap between who you are now and who you are becoming in Me. Acceptance trusts that I began this good work in you and am fully able to complete it—and looks to partner with Me in that process.

Beloved, We are the safest, kindest, gentlest, most gracious place you could ever know. In the warmth of Our acceptance, you can relax.

Receive Our permission to be yourself; to come to Us without fear, without shame, without condemnation because the most vital part of this process is for you to be open, honest, and truthful about where you are now and what you are learning.

I seek to replace shame with boldness so that you can come to My throne of grace to receive mercy and help at your point of need. My acceptance makes Me approachable. So, I want you to approach!

My loving-kindnesses indeed never cease; therefore, you will never be consumed because My compassions never fail! This creates the safety to be yourself and to experience your life in Christ, to live in awareness of Our presence in ways that will astonish you.

You'll hear the sounds of chains dropping all around your life in Christ—to live in awareness of Our presence in ways that will astonish you.

That is the starting point for all process—to know that you are accepted in the Beloved. To be set free from striving and live in the same peace that We have about your life.

I know the plans I have for you. I know how to walk with you in them. You're just walking with Me; feeling My acceptance, My smile, My delight in being with you; watching how I do life; and then following Me.

> With your hand in Mine, you will relax and My peace will rise in you. When you're in peace, you can hear. When you're at rest, your sensitivity to My Spirit increases.
>
> Allow acceptance to become a consistent part of our process of growth as you delight in our fellowship together. Remember that one of My titles is I AM, and I AM is always delighted to be in you and with you.
>
> Amen.

Jesus invites us to keep company with Him, living as much-loved children of God, and to learn how to live freely and lightly, because Jesus didn't die to give you value—He died because you are valuable.

> *Jesus resumed talking to the people, but now tenderly. "The Father has given me all these things to do and say. This is a unique Father-Son operation, coming out of Father and Son intimacies and knowledge. No one knows the Son the way the Father does, nor the Father the way the Son does. But I'm not keeping it to myself; I'm ready to go over it line by line with anyone willing to listen.*
>
> *"Are you tired? Worn out? Burned out on religion? Come to me. Get away with me and you'll recover your life. I'll show you how to take a real rest. Walk with me and work with me—watch how I do it. Learn the unforced rhythms of grace. I won't lay anything heavy or ill-fitting on you. Keep company with me and you'll learn to live freely and lightly"* (Matthew 11:27-30 MSG).

Primarily, we are learning to love ourselves as He loves us, receiving the dignity and glory He has bestowed on us.

> *I in them and You in Me, that they may be perfected in unity, so that the world may know that You sent Me, and loved them, even as You have loved Me* (John 17:23).
>
> *But in all these things we overwhelmingly conquer through Him who loved us. For I am convinced that neither death, nor life, nor angels, nor principalities, nor things present, nor things to come, nor powers, nor height, nor depth, nor any other created thing, will be able to separate us from the love of God, which is in Christ Jesus our Lord* (Romans 8:37-39).
>
> *Blessed is a man who perseveres under trial; for once he has been approved, he will receive the crown of life which the Lord has promised to those who love Him* (James 1:12).
>
> *We know love by this, that He laid down His life for us; and we ought to lay down our lives for the brethren* (1 John 3:16).
>
> *We have come to know and have believed the love which God has for us. God is love, and the one who abides in love abides in God, and God abides in him* (1 John 4:16).

The journey of maturing as a disciple is the discovery of who we are in Christ based on what we have received, not what we have earned.

I am not a sinner saved by grace. I am much more than that. I am a son/child of God.

> *For you are all sons of God through faith in Christ Jesus* (Galatians 3:26).

I have received forgiveness for all my sins—past, present, and future—as well as an inheritance.

> *To open their eyes so that they may turn from darkness to light and from the dominion of Satan to God, that they may receive forgiveness of sins and an inheritance among those who have been sanctified by faith in Me* (Acts 26:18).

> *When you were dead in your transgressions and the uncircumcision of your flesh, He made you alive together with Him, having forgiven us all our transgressions, having canceled out the certificate of debt consisting of decrees against us, which was hostile to us; and He has taken it out of the way, having nailed it to the cross* (Colossians 2:13-14).
>
> *Giving thanks to the Father, who has qualified us to share in the inheritance of the saints in Light* (Colossians 1:12).

Here it is significant to note that I am qualified by God to receive this inheritance. Our life experience is one of doing something to be qualified. I have a university degree that qualified me to be a social worker. I earned the qualification through study, writing essays, sitting exams, and undertaking placements in real-life settings. However, I received an inheritance when my mother died, being qualified when she gave birth to me and by being included in her will. As her will was read, I learned what I had received, not earned. So it is with my inheritance through Jesus—I need to read His word to see what I have received.

My inheritance through Jesus enables me to be a partaker of His divine nature. To be conformed to His image so that I can impact my world like He impacted His.

> *Grace and peace be multiplied to you in the knowledge of God and of Jesus our Lord; seeing that His divine power has granted to us everything pertaining to life and godliness, through the true knowledge of Him who called us by His own glory and excellence. For by these He has granted to us His precious and magnificent promises, so that by them you may become partakers of the divine nature, having escaped the corruption that is in the world by lust* (2 Peter 1:2-4).

> *For those whom He foreknew, He also predestined to become conformed to the image of His Son, so that He would be the firstborn among many brethren* (Romans 8:29).
>
> *Truly, truly, I say to you, he who believes in Me, the works that I do, he will do also; and greater works than these he will do; because I go to the Father* (John 14:12).

This is possible because of what I have been given through being crucified with Christ and the faith I place in Him.

> *I have been crucified with Christ; and it is no longer I who live, but Christ lives in me; and the life which I now live in the flesh I live by faith in the Son of God, who loved me and gave Himself up for me* (Galatians 2:20).

I have the mind of Christ.

> *For who has known the mind of the Lord, that he will instruct Him? But we have the mind of Christ* (1 Corinthians 2:16).

I have His peace that can still a storm.

> *Peace I leave with you; My peace I give to you; not as the world gives do I give to you. Do not let your heart be troubled, nor let it be fearful* (John 14:27).

I have His joy to find a way through every circumstance.

> *These things I have spoken to you so that My joy may be in you, and that your joy may be made full* (John 15:11).

I have received His love and am loved by the Father as He loves Jesus.

> *I in them and You in Me, that they may be perfected in unity, so that the world may know that You sent Me, and loved them, even as You have loved Me* (John 17:23).

I am in a line of succession where I have access to everything I need for every situation.

> *So then let no one boast in men. For all things belong to you, whether Paul or Apollos or Cephas or the world or life or death or things present or things to come; all things belong to you, and you belong to Christ; and Christ belongs to God* (1 Corinthians 3:21-23).

I have received every spiritual blessing and am seated in heavenly places.

> *Blessed be the God and Father of our Lord Jesus Christ, who has blessed us with every spiritual blessing in the heavenly places in Christ* (Ephesians 1:3).
>
> *And raised us up with Him, and seated us with Him in the heavenly places in Christ Jesus* (Ephesians 2:6).

I can be led by the Spirit at all times.

> *I will ask the Father, and He will give you another Helper, that He may be with you forever; that is the Spirit of truth, whom the world cannot receive, because it does not see Him or know Him, but you know Him because He abides with you and will be in you* (John 14:16-17).

As a New Testament believer, the Father, Son, and Holy Spirit are all working together with a deep commitment to helping us grow up into the image of Christ so that His Kingdom comes through us to those around us. When Paul pointed toward the behavior of a follower of Jesus, he was not calling us to *act* or *do* better. Instead, he was leading us to a new way of living based in Christ, not in ourselves. For example, the fruit of the Spirit—love, joy, peace, patience, kindness, generosity, faithfulness, gentleness, and self-control—are fruit born out from where we are planted. Not from effort or trying harder. They are a consequence of our relationship with love, for God is Love.

When Paul wrote to the Romans, he expressed it this way:

> *Therefore do not let what is for you a good thing be spoken of as evil; for the kingdom of God is not eating and drinking, but righteousness and peace and joy in the Holy Spirit. For he who in this way serves Christ is acceptable to God and approved by men* (Romans 14:16-18).

The context here in Romans is the use of rules. A prescribed set of behaviors being used to judge others spiritually is not the way of the Kingdom. Nor is it the way to serve Jesus. That is, the Kingdom of God is not about a focus on behavior, eating, and drinking—our actions. The Kingdom of God is about living in what we have received:

> *He made Him who knew no sin to be sin on our behalf, so that we might become the righteousness of God in Him* (2 Corinthians 5:21).
>
> *Peace I leave with you; My peace I give to you; not as the world gives do I give to you. Do not let your heart be troubled, nor let it be fearful* (John 14:27).
>
> *These things I have spoken to you so that My joy may be in you, and that your joy may be made full* (John 15:11).

We have already received righteousness, peace, and joy. Now we are learning how to live from what is ours through Jesus. As we serve Jesus from what is ours, this results in us being "acceptable to God and approved by men." Paul's goal was not to get us to *act* differently but to *be* different in our becoming and our transformation.

> *I have been crucified with Christ; and it is no longer I who live, but Christ lives in me; and the life which I now live in*

the flesh I live by faith in the Son of God, who loved me and gave Himself up for me (Galatians 2:20).

That is, we are abiding in the same love and life that Jesus received from the Father, with the result that compassion, kindness, and gentleness begin to flow through and from us. Paul is not giving us a new set of ethical rules, he is calling us to live from—not toward—our new identity.

I am intrigued by the way Jesus took matters of ethical behavior. He turned the conversation away from being centered on getting issues resolved based on a correct point of view, toward resolutions based on a foundation of love. For example, the proper grounds for divorce (see Matt. 19:3-12); the current attitude toward the government (see Matt. 22:17-22); the appropriate way to handle adultery (see John 8:2-11); and the right rules to keep on the Sabbath (see Luke 6:1-11). In approaching ethical matters this way, Jesus demonstrates part of the learning we are to embrace. That is, to stop relying on our judgments about what is right and wrong in our relationships with others. To draw on the abundant life found in walking with and in God.

It is a great joy to keep company with Jesus as a much-loved child who has inherited so much. It is a joy because we are unlearning the ways of the old self and learning the ways of the new self in a loving relationship.

> *For I am convinced that neither death, nor life, nor angels, nor principalities, nor things present, nor things to come, nor powers, nor height, nor depth, nor any other created thing, will be able to separate us from the love of God, which is in Christ Jesus our Lord* (Romans 8:38-39).

Paul helps us to explore this approach to our learning, and unlearning, in Colossians 2 and 3. In chapter 3 we read:

> *Therefore if you have been raised up with Christ, keep seeking the things above, where Christ is, seated at the right hand of God* (Colossians 3:1).

Paul begins this verse with the word *therefore*. Whenever you see the word *therefore*, you need to ask, "What is the therefore there for?!" Remember, Paul didn't write his letters with chapters, verses, and headings. He wrote a letter for the purpose of instruction through conversation. His letters represent a flow of ideas that build on one another. The *therefore* highlights that the next thought is connected to what he has previously been writing about.

To understand the *therefore* in Colossians 3:1, we need to go back:

> *For I want you to know how great a struggle I have on your behalf and for those who are at Laodicea, and for all those who have not personally seen my face, that their hearts may be encouraged, having been knit together in love, and attaining to all the wealth that comes from the full assurance of understanding, resulting in a true knowledge of God's mystery, that is, Christ Himself* (Colossians 2:1-2).

Paul is letting the Colossians—and us—know that he is laboring, striving, and in a great struggle to help us understand *"a true knowledge of God's mystery, that is, Christ Himself."* Wherever there is a mystery, there will be persuasive arguments and prevailing philosophies that compete to bring some answers to the mystery.

> *I say this so that no one will delude you with persuasive argument* (Colossians 2:4).
>
> *See to it that no one takes you captive through philosophy and empty deception, according to the tradition of men, according to the elementary principles of the world, rather than according to Christ* (Colossians 2:8).

Paul is not only drawing attention to the fact that there is a fight but also distinctly identifying what needs to be learned and unlearned.

Paul wants us to *"walk in Him, having been firmly rooted and now being built up in Him and established in your faith"* (Col. 2:6-7). From verse nine to fifteen, Paul clearly establishes who Jesus is, who we are in Him, and what He accomplished for us and in us.

> *For in Him all the fullness of Deity dwells in bodily form, and in Him you have been made complete, and He is the head over all rule and authority; and in Him you were also circumcised with a circumcision made without hands, in the removal of the body of the flesh by the circumcision of Christ; having been buried with Him in baptism, in which you were also raised up with Him through faith in the working of God, who raised Him from the dead. When you were dead in your transgressions and the uncircumcision of your flesh, He made you alive together with Him, having forgiven us all our transgressions, having canceled out the certificate of debt consisting of decrees against us, which was hostile to us; and He has taken it out of the way, having nailed it to the cross. When He had disarmed the rulers and authorities, He made a public display of them, having triumphed over them through Him* (Colossians 2:9-15).

Again, it is crucial that we grasp the depth and significance of being forgiven all our transgressions. Our familiarity with a verse like Second Corinthians 5:17 can dull our insight into the truth that our "old self" has been nailed to the cross.

> *Therefore if anyone is in Christ, he is a new creature; the old things passed away; behold, new things have come.*

The death of our old nature is graphically described by Paul when he writes:

> *Or do you not know that all of us who have been baptized into Christ Jesus have been baptized into His death? Therefore we have been buried with Him through baptism into death, so that as Christ was raised from the dead through the glory of the Father, so we too might walk in newness of life* (Romans 6:3-4).

Paul then goes on to help us see clearly the day-to-day consequences of being a new creation. That the old nature has passed away and we are to live from our new nature.

> *Now if we have died with Christ, we believe that we shall also live with Him* (Romans 6:8).

Our new nature is, "Christ in you, the hope of glory." We no longer have a sin nature, but we do wrestle with sin habits. We do have negative emotions, fear, anxiety, memories of hurts, and wounds that were formed by the corruption of darkness. These are normal in the flesh but are abnormal in Christ. We are being renewed by the Word and the Spirit as what is abnormal comes under the life of Jesus within. A renewal to receive the full transformation and freedom that Jesus has won for us.

Paul wants the Colossians, and us, to learn and know we have right standing and are in right relationship with God as His forgiven children because of our faith in the death and resurrection of Jesus. That is who we are, have become, and will be as Christ-followers. Paul then turns his attention to the importance of unlearning the persuasive argument that right standing and relationship with God are based on correct behavior—that is, how we act.

> *Therefore no one is to act as your judge in regard to food or drink or in respect to a festival or a new moon or a Sabbath day—things which are a mere shadow of what is to come; but the substance belongs to Christ. Let no one keep defrauding*

you of your prize by delighting in self-abasement and the worship of the angels, taking his stand on visions he has seen, inflated without cause by his fleshly mind, and not holding fast to the head, from whom the entire body, being supplied and held together by the joints and ligaments, grows with a growth which is from God.

If you have died with Christ to the elementary principles of the world, why, as if you were living in the world, do you submit yourself to decrees, such as, "Do not handle, do not taste, do not touch!" (which all refer to things destined to perish with use)—*in accordance with the commandments and teachings of men? These are matters which have, to be sure, the appearance of wisdom in self-made religion and self-abasement and severe treatment of the body, but are of no value against fleshly indulgence* (Colossians 2:16-23).

Having established how to walk in Him, Paul begins Colossians 3:1 with *therefore*. That is, knowing that we walk with God and He walks with us based on faith practice, "keep seeking the things above." Be focused on spiritual realities and truths that originate in heaven to frame your thinking, not the distortions that your circumstances or other people try to impose.

Set your mind on the things above, not on the things that are on earth (Colossians 3:2).

This is all possible and appropriate because:

For you have died and your life is hidden with Christ in God. When Christ, who is our life, is revealed, then you also will be revealed with Him in glory (Colossians 3:3-4).

Paul then introduces another *therefore*. We are to consider our old ways as no longer having power over us. To learn, through transformation and renewal by the Spirit and the Word, how to put off behavior that does not reflect the image of Jesus through changing what we believe.

> *And have put on the new self who is being renewed to a true knowledge according to the image of the One who created him* (Colossians 3:10).

Paul then wants us to learn to abide in the truth of who we are in Christ so that we can grow up into all He has called us to be.

> *So, as those who have been chosen of God, holy and beloved, put on a heart of compassion, kindness, humility, gentleness and patience; bearing with one another, and forgiving each other, whoever has a complaint against anyone; just as the Lord forgave you, so also should you. Beyond all these things put on love, which is the perfect bond of unity. Let the peace of Christ rule in your hearts, to which indeed you were called in one body; and be thankful. Let the word of Christ richly dwell within you, with all wisdom teaching and admonishing one another with psalms and hymns and spiritual songs, singing with thankfulness in your hearts to God. Whatever you do in word or deed, do all in the name of the Lord Jesus, giving thanks through Him to God the Father* (Colossians 3:12-17).

Here Paul is asking us to practice who we have become. We have become chosen, holy, and beloved, and from these realities Christ in us will guide us to His lifestyle. As He was in the world, so we are to be in the world (see 1 John 4:17). The Holy Spirit is consistently inviting us into their lifestyle because:

> *I have been crucified with Christ; and it is no longer I who live, but Christ lives in me; and the life which I now live in*

the flesh I live by faith in the Son of God, who loved me and gave Himself up for me (Galatians 2:20).

There is the opportunity to be renewed through everything we face. Jesus is with us, as He is in us, in all of life's circumstances. He lives in us to build us into His image and likeness. While our circumstances engage us, we are to abide and live in Jesus through them. We partner with God's development of us by being focused on the things above and that we have inherited. He is with us in our lowest places to empower us and raise us up. He is dedicated to filling up what is missing in our experience of Him and His love.

So we can approach our learning from the position of total acceptance and being fully forgiven as the righteousness of God in Christ Jesus to see how God sees us.

> *Blessed be the God and Father of our Lord Jesus Christ, who has blessed us with every spiritual blessing in the heavenly places in Christ, just as He chose us in Him before the foundation of the world, that we would be holy and blameless before Him. In love He predestined us to adoption as sons through Jesus Christ to Himself, according to the kind intention of His will, to the praise of the glory of His grace, which He freely bestowed on us in the Beloved. In Him we have redemption through His blood, the forgiveness of our trespasses, according to the riches of His grace which He lavished on us. In all wisdom and insight He made known to us the mystery of His will, according to His kind intention which He purposed in Him with a view to an administration suitable to the fullness of the times, that is, the summing up of all things in Christ, things in the heavens and things on the earth. In Him also we have obtained an inheritance, having been predestined according to His purpose who works all things after the counsel of His will, to the end that we who were the first to hope in*

> *Christ would be to the praise of His glory. In Him, you also, after listening to the message of truth, the gospel of your salvation—having also believed, you were sealed in Him with the Holy Spirit of promise, who is given as a pledge of our inheritance, with a view to the redemption of God's own possession, to the praise of His glory* (Ephesians 1:3-14).

We are learning to walk with God knowing that He calls us up into our righteousness and doesn't call us out to punish us for the wrong choices we make.

> *But now I am going to Him who sent Me; and none of you asks Me, "Where are You going?" But because I have said these things to you, sorrow has filled your heart. But I tell you the truth, it is to your advantage that I go away; for if I do not go away, the Helper will not come to you; but if I go, I will send Him to you. And He, when He comes, will convict the world concerning sin and righteousness and judgment; concerning sin, because they do not believe in Me; and concerning righteousness, because I go to the Father and you no longer see Me; and concerning judgment, because the ruler of this world has been judged* (John 16:5-11).

We are learning to become like the person He is through Spirit-led transformation and knowing who He is for us personally.

> *For those whom He foreknew, He also predestined to become conformed to the image of His Son, so that He would be the firstborn among many brethren* (Romans 8:29).
>
> *After you have suffered for a little while, the God of all grace, who called you to His eternal glory in Christ, will Himself perfect, confirm, strengthen and establish you* (1 Peter 5:10).

Paul has some insightful thoughts in Romans 8 regarding what to unlearn and learn when we are faced with suffering, so that we walk with Jesus into the freedom He has won for us.

Beginning in Romans 8:31, Paul writes, *"What then shall we say to these things?"* Our question needs to be, what is Paul referring to when he says "these things"? Again, we need to go back into the text as Paul is building a perspective for us to understand.

Romans 8:1 is a beginning point for the "these things" Paul is referring to.

> *Therefore there is now no condemnation for those who are in Christ Jesus* (Romans 8:1).

Alongside of no condemnation, Paul insists that we are set free (see Rom. 8:2). And that Christ is in you, meaning we can live according to the Spirit and be led by the Spirit, resulting in us being adopted as children of God (see Rom. 8:10,13,16). Interestingly, with all of these things in our favor, we are still going to suffer:

> *For I consider that the sufferings of this present time are not worthy to be compared with the glory that is to be revealed to us* (Romans 8:18).

Not only are we going to suffer, but we will also have to face our weaknesses.

> *In the same way the Spirit also helps our weakness; for we do not know how to pray as we should, but the Spirit Himself intercedes for us with groanings too deep for words* (Romans 8:26).

However, the combination of the favor we have received and the struggles we face can come together in God so that we are "conformed to the image of His Son." It is in this context of life's realities where Paul indicates that our role is to speak to what we are facing. We do this in such a way that we become one of the many brethren Jesus was the firstborn of.

Paul sees that the struggles and weaknesses we face can trigger negative thoughts, beliefs, and self-talk. This can lead us back into rule-based, fear-generating postures that lead to slavery. When we believe things have gone wrong, it presupposes that we have missed what was right.

Let me explain. Romans 8:31-32 says:

> *If God is for us, who is against us? He who did not spare His own Son, but delivered Him over for us all, how will He not also with Him freely give us all things?* (Romans 8:31-32)

When *things go wrong*, we interpret something has come against us that we are either responsible for or need to fix. However, Paul is calling us to unlearn a binary expectation that my wrong behavior has brought this consequence upon me. Instead, he wants us to learn that if *"while we were yet sinners, Christ died for us"* (Rom. 5:8), then God is no longer relating to us based on our behavior. He relates to us based on who He has decided to be for us: *"He who did not spare His own Son."*

Next, Romans 8:33 says:

> *Who will bring a charge against God's elect? God is the one who justifies.*

A charge, either in our self-talk or from someone else, is an accusation aimed at who you are and comes against your identity—that is, "*I am wrong.*" Paul is urging us to unlearn defining ourselves by what others say is wrong with us or their judgments on what they value as appropriate. Instead, he wants us to learn to see that Jesus has justified us. He sees our potential and is working toward our freedom.

> *It was for freedom that Christ set us free; therefore keep standing firm and do not be subject again to a yoke of slavery* (Galatians 5:1).

Next, Romans 8:34 says:

> *Who is the one who condemns? Christ Jesus is He who died, yes, rather who was raised, who is at the right hand of God, who also intercedes for us.*

Condemnation, either in our self-talk or from someone else, is disapproval or criticism aimed at what we do, our behavior, declaring that *"My behavior is wrong."* Paul is saying to unlearn defining ourselves by behavior management based on rules and laws. Instead, he wants us to learn to see that Jesus is asking, on our behalf, that we receive grace in our times of need. Grace is helping us to become who we are in Christ, not requiring that we try harder to behave according to a standard.

Finally, Romans 8:35 and 37 say:

> *Who will separate us from the love of Christ? Will tribulation, or distress, or persecution, or famine, or nakedness, or peril, or sword?*
>
> *But in all these things we overwhelmingly conquer through Him who loved us.*

Here in this verse of being "wrong in my *circumstances*," Paul is calling us to unlearn that God is upset with us and using circumstances to punish us. Instead, we are to learn that because God loves us as He loves Jesus, we can place our confidence in the truth that we have always been loved and will always be loved because God is love (see 1 John 4:16).

We are learning to live our whole lives in response to the love of God. We are learning to live from who we are in Christ and not toward some set of behavioral expectations. Our learning is being built on the foundation of self-awareness and personal responsibility. That is, I came to faith by becoming self-aware that my relationship with God was broken. I then took responsibility for this breakdown by praying that my sin would be forgiven and declaring that I would put my trust in Jesus. I came into a relationship with God through self-awareness and personal responsibility, so all growth in that relationship will begin with the same principles.

This is supported in Philippians 2:12-13:

> *So then, my beloved, just as you have always obeyed, not as in my presence only, but now much more in my absence, work out your salvation with fear and trembling; for it is God who is at work in you, both to will and to work for His good pleasure.*

Here Paul is calling us to work out, or understand, what actually took place in you and for you when you were born again. As you purposefully explore these realities, the Holy Spirit will lead and empower your journey of discovery. Then you can serve Him and represent Him well and give Jesus His full reward.

Paul describes the learning when he declares that he is now living under the law of the Spirit of life in Christ Jesus and not the law of sin and death, resulting in condemnation (see Rom. 8:2). We are confidently practicing a lifestyle that anticipates the Holy Spirit will be pursuing His work in our soul—our mind, will, and emotions. The Helper, Comforter, and Counselor will bring *mind* transformation through revelation, *will* transformation through power encounters, and *emotional* transformation through experiences with God's love.

Jesus made it so clear that this is the Holy Spirit's delight and joy. To guide us into all truth, disclose what is to come, and disclose the person of Jesus.

> *But when He, the Spirit of truth, comes, He will guide you into all the truth; for He will not speak on His own initiative, but whatever He hears, He will speak; and He will disclose to you what is to come. He will glorify Me, for He will take of Mine and will disclose it to you. All things that the Father has are Mine; therefore I said that He takes of Mine and will disclose it to you* (John 16:13-15).

The Holy Spirit is motivated to empower us and train us in and through a process while never leaving or forsaking us.

> *I will ask the Father, and He will give you another Helper, that He may be with you forever; that is the Spirit of truth, whom the world cannot receive, because it does not see Him or know Him, but you know Him because He abides with you and will be in you* (John 14:16-17).

The Holy Spirit is actively leading us to lay aside our sin habits and to elevate us into who we are in Christ. He wants us to fully comprehend how we are seen, known, and accepted by them.

> *But the Helper, the Holy Spirit, whom the Father will send in My name, He will teach you all things, and bring to your remembrance all that I said to you* (John 14:26).
>
> *When the Helper comes, whom I will send to you from the Father, that is the Spirit of truth who proceeds from the Father, He will testify about Me, and you will testify also, because you have been with Me from the beginning* (John 15:26-27).

Our confidence is expressed by sitting with Holy Spirit and asking questions. Jesus taught in parables as He wanted us to understand through questions of discovery what His intended message was in the parable. He wanted to teach us how to engage and think, not just what to think. The Father entered the Garden of Eden after Adam and Eve's sin. He asked two questions to promote self-awareness for the outcome of personal responsibility. Relationships flourish and deepen through understanding, which is always preceded by asking questions.

The journey of knowing God, knowing ourselves, and experiencing the life-giving impact that Jesus offers is released by asking Holy Spirit questions. These questions accept that the heart has reasons the head does not understand, but Holy Spirit is the one who does understand the reasons.

Here is a list of life processing questions for you to bring to Holy Spirit that Graham Cooke has developed:

- If Jesus were looking out through my eyes, how would He see my current situation?
- How do I want to partner with God as He develops me?
- What does this situation mean for our relationship, God?
- What am I believing God for in my current situation?
- If Jesus were looking out through my eyes, how would He see this person I'm dealing with or this battle that I am in?
- How would the Holy Spirit turn this problem into a possibility?
- How is the favor of God working to my benefit in this situation?
- What new lenses and mind-sets should I be viewing my current situation through?

- If I am to grow up into all things in Christ, what must I unlearn from the ways of the world in order to learn the Way, the Truth, and the Life of the Kingdom?
- What new truth is God replacing in my life?
- When is what is true not the Truth?
- What am I focusing on most in my thinking?
- What opportunity for development is God orchestrating in my life right now?
- How is the fruit of the Holy Spirit an effective weapon?
- How do I count the cost of moving forward with God?
- What new freedom must I explore now?
- How can I be sensitive to the Holy Spirit?
- What does it mean to dream with God?
- What good things are already in me?
- How do we practically love those who don't like us?
- If I believe what God is saying, what are the outcomes for me?

All the above assumes that followers of Jesus have decided to pursue their spiritual growth with intent and determination. They desire to purposefully embrace a lifestyle of relational learning with Jesus in life's circumstances. They practice communion with Jesus as a lifestyle, being positioned in the affections of God and revealing God's nature in every circumstance.

> *For in Him we live and move and exist, as even some of your own poets have said, "For we also are His children"* (Acts 17:28).

A lifestyle of relational learning has grasped the reality of being chosen, holy, and beloved. As we are seen by God as blameless, He is not judging us. Instead, He is highlighting, with kindness, what is missing. God talks us into something, not out of something. He speaks to us through how He sees us so that we can move out of what is imprisoning us. Once we have placed our trust in Jesus, He convicts us of our righteousness (see John 16:10). He calls us up in our behavior into who we already are in Him—the righteousness of God.

> *He made Him who knew no sin to be sin on our behalf, so that we might become the righteousness of God in Him* (2 Corinthians 5:21).

For example, someone trapped in the prison of pornography, seeking comfort to their pain and brokenness, is missing the understanding of the freedom found in purity. The Holy Spirit shines light onto the addiction to bring about self-awareness and personal responsibility to motivate a response of coming before the throne of grace in a time of need (see Heb. 4:16). It is here that the all-powerful, all-knowing comforter brings help and counsel. He shows us God's path of redemption from the influence of past responses that the old man developed to cope.

God has not just declared that we are not guilty. He went one step further and has declared us innocent. Love to God means 100 percent forgiven. What God is for us, we are to be for others. So for us to love as He loves, we need to live a life knowing that because we are 100 percent forgiven we need to forgive others (and ourselves) 100 percent. To love like this has everything to do with desire, not performance. Desire is translated into a decision to think and see life in the same way God does, knowing that if He is love, I am love, because He is in me.

We are called to be single-minded as He is single-minded. Therefore, we can't let our mind-set toward another be influenced by their behavior because that will result in judgment, criticism, and being double-minded. We can't judge people and still expect to have fellowship with them based on love. Our mind-set needs to be influenced by the love God has for us because we live in the Kingdom of oneness.

We are to be for others what Jesus has been for us.

Summary

Jesus invites us to keep company with Him, living as much loved children and learning to live freely and lightly.

My inheritance through Jesus enables me to be a partaker of His divine nature, to be conformed to His image so that I can impact my world like He impacted His.

The Kingdom of God is not based on a focus on behavior; it is about living in what we have received.

True knowledge of God's mystery—that is, Christ Himself—is challenged by persuasive arguments and prevailing philosophies that, in turn, undermine how we walk with God.

We are to consider our old ways as no longer having power over us and to learn, through transformation and renewal by the Spirit and the Word, how to put off behavior that does not reflect the image of Jesus through changing what we believe.

We need to unlearn and learn how to walk with God to escape a rule-based posture when things go wrong, when my self-talk says I am wrong and/or my behavior is wrong, and something in my circumstances is wrong.

The journey of knowing God, knowing ourselves, and experiencing the life-giving impact that Jesus offers is released by asking questions of the Holy Spirit.

A lifestyle of relational learning has grasped the reality of being chosen, holy, and beloved.

Questions and Activity

1. How do you keep company with Jesus?
2. What would need to change for you to learn to live freely and lightly with Jesus?
3. Name five aspects of the inheritance you have received in Jesus and how they help you to change the world.
4. What do you have to unlearn to walk with God in confidence that He is with you, for you, and believes in you?

Note

1. Graham Cooke, "The Way God Walks with Us," https://www.brillianttv.com/the-way-god-walks-with-us.

Chapter Five

HIS GREAT GRACE

...Living from What We Have Received

THE STORYLINE OF *LES MISÉRABLES* IS A POWERFUL ILLUSTRATION of how grace helps us to live a life that honors, loves, and respects others, while contrasting it with the effects of being law-based.

> The convict Jean Valjean is released from a French prison after serving nineteen years for stealing a loaf of bread and for subsequent attempts to escape from prison. When Valjean arrives at the town of Digne, no one is willing to give him shelter because he is an ex-convict. Desperate, Valjean knocks on the door of M. Myriel, the kindly bishop of Digne. Myriel treats Valjean with kindness, and Valjean repays the bishop by stealing his silverware. When the police arrest Valjean, Myriel [motivated by the understanding of grace] covers for him, claiming that the silverware was a gift. The authorities release Valjean and Myriel makes him promise to become an honest man. Eager to fulfill his promise, Valjean masks his identity and enters the town of Montreuil-sur-mer. Under the assumed name of Madeleine, Valjean invents an ingenious manufacturing process that brings the town prosperity. He eventually becomes the town's mayor.

An act of grace releases transformation.

> Fantine, a young woman from Montreuil, lives in Paris. She falls in love with Tholomyès, a wealthy student who gets her pregnant and then abandons her. Fantine returns to her home village with her daughter, Cosette. On the way to Montreuil, however, Fantine realizes that she will never be able to find work if the townspeople know that she has an illegitimate child.
>
> …In Montreuil, Fantine finds work in Madeleine's factory. Fantine's coworkers find out about Cosette, however, and Fantine is fired. …Fantine resorts to prostitution to make ends meet. One night, Javert, Montreuil's police chief, arrests Fantine. She is to be sent to prison, but Madeleine intervenes. Fantine has fallen ill, and when she longs to see Cosette, Madeleine promises to send for her. First, however, he must contend with Javert, who has discovered Madeleine's criminal past. Javert tells Madeleine that a man has been accused of being Jean Valjean, and Madeleine confesses his true identity. Javert shows up to arrest Valjean.[1]

As Valjean becomes a man to release grace and mercy, he is confronted by law. Valjean is sent to prison, escapes, and purposefully sets out to be reunited with Cosette as Fantine has died. Cosette and Valjean move to Paris, where Javert finds them, and they must flee through the city at night. Grace, mercy, and the law again challenge one another.

Years later, Cosette falls in love with a young man named Marius, who learns of a plan by others to rob Valjean. Marius alerts the local police inspector, who turns out to be Javert, of the planned ambush and robbery. However, Valjean escapes before Javert can identify him.

Marius falls in with his fellow university students who have started a political uprising. Javert joins their ranks as a spy; however, his cover is exposed, and he is tied up as the army launches an attack on the students. Valjean arrives at the barricade to find Marius and sees Javert tied up and volunteers to execute him. However, when alone with Javert, Valjean instead secretly lets him go free. Mercy and grace triumph over judgment.

> As the army storms the barricade, Valjean grabs the wounded Marius and flees through the sewers. When Valjean emerges hours later, Javert immediately arrests him. Valjean pleads with Javert to let him take the dying Marius to Marius's grandfather. Javert agrees. Javert feels tormented, torn between his duty to his profession and the debt he owes Valjean for saving his life. Ultimately, Javert lets Valjean go and throws himself into the river, where he drowns.[2]

Valjean was able to see his need to respond to grace. Javert was unable to embrace grace as his worldview was defined by a commitment to law and judgment. Valjean was able to live from what he had received. At the same time, Javert was unable to embrace the reality of mercy triumphing over judgment.

Grace is the empowering presence of God. It is the strength God gives us to live from the inheritance of being in Christ and be like Jesus in every circumstance through life. It's the strength God lends to those who recognize their need for power other than their own to manage life from a Kingdom posture and perspective. This empowering presence is often not drawn upon by God's people as they remain unconvinced about who they really are and what inheritance they have received. Like Javert, they see it. Yet they fail to see that by placing their trust in Jesus, there is a completion rather than a commencement.

> *For if by the transgression of the one, death reigned through the one, much more those who receive the abundance of grace and of the gift of righteousness will reign in life through the One, Jesus Christ* (Romans 5:17).

The Christian life led from a sense of duty will gravitate to using the law—rules and regulations—to assess how well they and others are fulfilling what they believe is expected. They are intimidated by weakness as it undermines successfully following the rules. The sense of duty leads to the belief that they are responsible to "get it right," and as a consequence they lean into their own strength. Paul, on the other hand, put no confidence in his own ability and through humility that engendered surrender declared:

> *And He has said to me, "My grace is sufficient for you, for power is perfected in weakness." Most gladly, therefore, I will rather boast about my weaknesses, so that the power of Christ may dwell in me. Therefore I am well content with weaknesses, with insults, with distresses, with persecutions, with difficulties, for Christ's sake; for when I am weak, then I am strong* (2 Corinthians 12:9-10).

Grace is much more than unmerited favor. Grace is opposed to being earned, yet it celebrates effort. We are to grow in grace:

> *But grow in the grace and knowledge of our Lord and Savior Jesus Christ. To Him be the glory, both now and to the day of eternity. Amen* (2 Peter 3:18).

That is, through practice and application, we nurture the ability to surrender self-centered and self-reliant ways to the ways of God. We cherish absorbing all God is for us, knowing we are not expected to be and do, on our own, all God called us to. We are to follow Jesus to do life with Him.

Our capacity to live a fully surrendered life that leans into grace is greatly influenced by how we see or know God. Our response to relying on and living in grace is directly linked to how we see and experience the love God has for us.

John 14:15—*"If you love Me, you will keep My commandments"*—is often read through our view of God. When we are fully immersed in and living from what we have received, this Scripture is heard as a voice full of acceptance and warmth, declaring:

"If you love Me, you won't do anything to hurt Me."

The impact in our heart is that our relationship with God is based on love—we want to do everything possible to protect Him from being concerned for our well-being. We want to honor His Lordship through being submitted to His kind intentions. We want to bless His heart through pursuing a lifestyle of learning to live from what we have received.

However, there are other ways that people experience God that lead them away from relying on His great grace to live from what we have received. They hear a different voice when Jesus says, *"If you love Me, you will keep my commandments."*

Some people view God as inspecting and demanding. The voice they hear when Jesus says, *"If you love Me, you will keep my commandments,"* has a questioning tone conveying that there is a test to be passed or a measurement to be taken:

"If you love Me, you will do what I say. I'll wait to see how much you really love Me based on what you do."

The impact on them is that God is continually recording what they do on His tally sheet. Good things too, but He inspects everything. He relates to us based on the number of positive and negative tally marks. Their perceived score determines how they feel loved by God and, in turn, how they relate to others and themselves. For example, they:

- Consider innocent comments or events to be personal attacks;
- Assume others are looking to find fault;
- A shared need from another elicits a defensive response;
- Underlying anxiety produces the tendency to "inspect" others;
- Spiritual life is robbed of joy and gratitude—not excited about prayer, meditation, or times with God.

Others view God as being disappointed in them. The voice they hear when Jesus says, *"If you love Me, you will keep My commandments,"* conveys a sense of failure and never being good enough:

> "If you really loved Me, then you would be able to keep My commandments. In fact, I have known all along you didn't really love Me, and what you did just proves that."

The impact on them is that they live out a Christian life with a sense of never measuring up. They perceive that God seldom likes what He sees and shakes His head in displeasure even when He notices attempts to live righteous lives. They are certain they will never make it, and no amount of right behavior is ever enough. This perception of the way they are loved by God manifests in behaviors such as:

- Having difficulty experiencing contentment and peace;
- Personal worth always in question;
- Striving to perform to feel worthy or not even trying;
- Using personal disappointment in coercive ways: "You *will* be at the service tonight, won't you?" or "I hope I can count on you to help with this event";

- Being hard to please—nothing is ever good enough in our relationship with others;
- Being driven by perfection;
- Seeking control.

Others view God as being distant. *"If you love Me, you will keep My commandments"* has a cold and distant tone, characterized by half-hearted enthusiasm or great indifference:

"Oh, it's you. If you love Me, wait over there until I've finished loving My favorite children."

The view is that God is only interested in "important" people and taking care of "important" things. Why would God who made the universe and has over seven billion people to deal with notice me? The concept of God as an aloof observer translates in relationships as:

- Approaching God with reluctance;
- Relating to others with emotional detachment, minimal intimacy, or fellowship;
- Finding trust difficult—resisting knowing and being known by others;
- An emotionally distant and uninvolved God requires self-reliance and love for Him motivated by a sense of duty or obligation;
- Difficulty in loving others in a relevant or meaningful way.

These views create lenses through which we approach and learn how to walk with God. Peter had a lens change when he met with Cornelius. He realized that his open vision of the forbidden animals on the white sheet was God indicating that the Gentiles were now welcome in the family of God. Yet Peter lost sight of this lens change experience and the revelation it released.

But when Cephas came to Antioch, I opposed him to his face, because he stood condemned. For prior to the coming of certain men from James, he used to eat with the Gentiles; but when they came, he began to withdraw and hold himself aloof, fearing the party of the circumcision. The rest of the Jews joined him in hypocrisy, with the result that even Barnabas was carried away by their hypocrisy. But when I saw that they were not straightforward about the truth of the gospel, I said to Cephas in the presence of all, "If you, being a Jew, live like the Gentiles and not like the Jews, how is it that you compel the Gentiles to live like Jews? (Galatians 2:11-14)

What we hear and what we become are two different things. Culturally, we have been trained to believe that if we understand something, we know it. That is, learning is about the accumulation of information. This perspective robs us of the depth of spiritual maturity that the Lord is offering us. To live in the fullness of our inheritance, we must acquire information that is applied through grace. It needs to be practiced, resulting in the transformation that grows or is established into a lifestyle.

Jesus' style of learning is captured when He said, *"Follow Me, and I will make…"* (Matt. 4:19). Similarly, Paul boldly declared, *"Be imitators of me, just as I also am of Christ"* (1 Cor. 11:1). That is, the focus is on relational learning, not our transactional and educational style of transmitting head knowledge. Head knowledge doesn't transform us as it removes a love for the presence of the teacher. Only the Holy Spirit can engage with the inner man of our heart and renew the mind at the same time.

Relational learning is often slow learning. If we are learning by following, then it is God who sets the pace. Our system of education presents material to be mastered in a specific time. The information covered is measured through assessment rather than establishing that it has been mastered through application.

Often, our learning with God is as much about unlearning as it is learning. He calls us to self-awareness and personal responsibility to recognize and change our old ways for His ways. What we thought was true is not true. We create internal prisons when we respond to life out of fear. When God shines His light on our fear and how it is harming us, we are set free.

> *There is no fear in love; but perfect love casts out fear, because fear involves punishment, and the one who fears is not perfected in love* (1 John 4:18).

The journey of discovery toward embracing the truth that we have been radically restored to oneness with God releases an awareness of acceptance, completion, and restoration of identity as an adopted child of God. In this environment of revelation, we can joyfully embrace the unlearning. Unfortunately, what we don't successfully unlearn will always necessitate revisiting. We need to rest in the place of knowing we are loved by a patient God who sees beyond the immediate wrestle of unlearning into a future marked by freedom.

We are to stay in tune with the Holy Spirit so that we are aligned to the process He has designed to help us to not just become a better version of our old self, but rather to benefit from the price Jesus paid to be conformed to His image. Therefore, we can only assess our growth, transformation, and maturity by who we are becoming, not the knowledge we have accumulated.

To move beyond a lens change into a lifestyle of being like Jesus, from where we live and move and draw our being, requires an understanding of spiritual formation. That is, the way God walks with us and introduces us to the way of Jesus.

The literature available on this topic is vast, extensive, draws on many spiritual traditions, and has significant historical roots. It is not my intention to offer any form of commentary of all that is available. Instead, I provide the following to assist your own research/voyage of discovery.

First, you may like to begin with these three books, which I found to be extremely helpful.

- *The Divine Conspiracy: Rediscovering Our Hidden Life in God* by Dallas Willard
- *Practicing the Way of Jesus: Life Together in the Kingdom of God* by Mark A. Scandrette
- *Discovering our Spiritual Identity: Practices for God's Beloved* by Trevor Hudson

Second, I offer the following as a framework for your journey of transformation and spiritual formation. Let's begin with several sayings I have accumulated over the years:

- Those who don't change their minds don't change anything.
- The unexamined life is not worth living.
- What got us *here* will not take us *there*.
- Success is not final, and failure is not fatal; it is the courage to continue that counts.

These sayings focus on the thought that there must be a hunger or appetite to pursue the practices and inhabit the process of formation.

If you know these things, you are blessed if you do them (John 13:17).

Do we have an appetite to grow up in Christ by becoming enthusiastic partakers of who we are in Christ? Are we open to the Spirit and the Word to persuade us of their value to restore everything about being an image-bearer of God Himself back to the way He originally intended us to be?

Will we prioritize a life of spiritual learning that includes seeing how God sees us; becoming the person He is; living in a close, loving relationship with God to both learn and unlearn; and discovering who Jesus wants to be for us personally?

The Lord's view of us includes our depiction as His workmanship.

> *For we are His workmanship, created in Christ Jesus for good works, which God prepared beforehand so that we would walk in them* (Ephesians 2:10).

The word *workmanship* in the original language means "poem or poetry." As God's workmanship, He is focused on our life becoming a place of beauty that resonates with His glory. A helpful illustration here is Michelangelo's observation that "every block of stone has a statue inside of it and it is the task of the sculptor to discover it." How true this is of the statue of David.

Paul understood the purpose of God's workmanship in our lives when he wrote:

> *So then, my beloved, just as you have always obeyed, not as in my presence only, but now much more in my absence, work out your salvation with fear and trembling; for it is God who is at work in you, both to will and to work for His good pleasure* (Philippians 2:12-13).

We are to be lifelong learners to discover the enormous value and expanse of our inheritance in Christ—that is, "work out your salvation."

> *Giving thanks to the Father, who has qualified us to share in the inheritance of the saints in Light* (Colossians 1:12).

We are to know that it is God Himself who has qualified us to live a life that is being conformed to the image of Jesus.

> *For those whom He foreknew, He also predestined to become conformed to the image of His Son, so that He would be the firstborn among many brethren* (Romans 8:29).

We are used to "earning" our qualifications through training and education—our performance. However, our life in God, along with its growth and maturity, begins with God's acceptance and adoption of us. It proceeds as He works to show us the sites in our belief systems that He will extend grace to for our transformation and freedom.

Paul declares that *"But now faith, hope, love, abide these three; but the greatest of these is love"* (1 Cor. 13:13). He begins this classic discourse on love in First Corinthians 13 with three verses that state that if ministry is accomplished in the absence of love, then our ministry efforts are questionable.

As previously discussed, the goal of all Paul's instruction and disciple-making was to see people grow and mature in the way they loved others. John considered the way we love others to be the primary and authentic indicator that we had accepted and were following Jesus (see 1 John 3:14). When Jesus observed that Zaccheus and his household had experienced salvation, it was based on a commitment to love and oneness (see Luke 19:8-9). Jesus rewrote the second of the two great commandments of the Old Testament from "Love one another as you love yourself" to "Love one another as I have loved you."

A significant and primary area of transformation and spiritual formation is in from where and how do we love God, others, and ourselves.

In Chapter One, I offered the thought that we have all learned to love ourselves, and therefore others and the Lord, based on performance. This is connected to the pursuit to belong, be significant, and be secure by answering the question: "What is right and required for acceptance?" Our answers are always based on things we need to *do*—performance.

Having concluded that we receive love and acceptance based on performance, we also give love based on performance. Not only that, but we also create Counselors of fear that speak to us in our self-talk that we are not and cannot be the person required to be accepted. For me, in my family of origin I decided that to be accepted and loved I needed to be a good boy and not get anything wrong. I created in my self-talk and imagination a fear of failure, fear of rejection, fear of being taken advantage of, and fear of being misunderstood.

When revelation and recognition combine, the process of transformation can begin. These are some of the keys I learned on my own journey.

John confidently asserts that:

> *There is no fear in love; but perfect love casts out fear, because fear involves punishment, and the one who fears is not perfected in love* (1 John 4:18).

Where fear is in our lives, we are yet to experience the love of God through an encounter with the Word and Spirit that transforms us.

> *And to know the love of Christ which surpasses knowledge, that you may be filled up to all the fullness of God* (Ephesians 3:19).

We know fear is present when the circumstances of life and/or our relationships squeeze us and "Jesus juice" does not come out! The promise, however, is that we can be filled up to the fullness of God, experiencing freedom from our social and personal fears through knowing how much Jesus loves us.

While this is true, it is by no means automatic through acquiring the head knowledge that "Jesus loves me." There is a process of discovery and exchange that must be entered into and walked out over time. Remember, spiritual learning is slow learning and measured by transformation.

What is an entry point into the process of discovery and exchange? Jesus provides a clue as to where to find this entry point. I believe this has the potential to reveal the site for freedom and change in the area(s) of our lives He is highlighting to us.

> *Jesus answered them, "Do you now believe? Behold, an hour is coming, and has already come, for you to be scattered, each to his own home, and to leave Me alone; and yet I am not alone, because the Father is with Me. These things I have spoken to you, so that in Me you may have peace. In the world you have tribulation, but take courage; I have overcome the world"* (John 16:31-33).

Previously we noted that the word *tribulation* here means inner turmoil. In this context, through self-awareness and personal responsibility, it is possible to observe and monitor our own feelings when life throws up its challenges. To discover our reactions and responses that do not emulate Jesus. Inner turmoil is always going to be a site for transformation and freedom if we can only be humble and willing to own it as our "stuff" so that we can come before the throne of grace in our time of need (see Heb. 4:16).

Jesus offers us a place of transformation. He will enable an exchange of inner turmoil for His peace based on revelation in our hearts that the Father is always with us (John 16:23). Paul builds on Jesus' encouragement when he notes:

> *And not only this, but we also exult in our tribulations, knowing that tribulation brings about perseverance; and*

perseverance, proven character; and proven character, hope; and hope does not disappoint, because the love of God has been poured out within our hearts through the Holy Spirit who was given to us (Romans 5:3-5).

The word here for tribulation has the same meaning of "inner turmoil" as in John 16:33 above. Paul enthusiastically calls us to "exult" in our inner turmoil. We are to celebrate the discovery of our sufferings and weaknesses—as children of God—as they are exposed by the Spirit and Word to help us be conformed to the image of Jesus. This happens as we, from a Kingdom perspective, manage the charges, condemnation, and uncertainty they generate in our self-talk (Rom. 8:14-39).

Not only are we to completely embrace our inner turmoil, but we are also to persevere in the process. The Lord will lead us through to release us into His freedom and His ways. Our perseverance sees the characteristics of the Godhead formed in us so that we can prove the character of Jesus is available to all. As others observe the changes in us, it generates hope that they—in their struggles—can encounter the love, acceptance, and freedom we have received from Jesus. In so doing, we learn to love others the same way Jesus loves us.

As we stay the course of spiritual formation through enthusiastic perseverance, it can be expected that the Lord will challenge us. There are three areas of our inner worlds concerning the specific issues He is at work in. Paul identifies the focus of the Spirit and Word in our transformation when he writes:

Therefore I urge you, brethren, by the mercies of God, to present your bodies a living and holy sacrifice, acceptable to God, which is your spiritual service of worship. And do not be conformed to this world, but be transformed by the renewing of your mind, so that you may prove what the will of God is, that which is good and acceptable and perfect (Romans 12:1-2).

What are the areas of your inner world Paul is pointing to here? The answer is found where he writes *"present your bodies a living and holy sacrifice, acceptable to God."* Here, Paul is drawing on his experience as a Pharisee. The temple sacrifice of a lamb was made holy and acceptable to God through three things that were administered to the dead animal. Paul is indicating that being transformed through the renewing of the mind requires us to present our lives in the same way as the sacrificial lamb.

The first required activity that made the lamb holy and acceptable was the removal of its head. In the Bible, the head is always synonymous with the site of authority. As "lords," we have established our own kingdoms centered on self-reliance and effort. Our personal kingdoms are ruled from what we choose to believe. To be a living sacrifice that is holy and acceptable to God, we must yield our authority in every area of our life. We must recognize God's ways as the Lord of lords and the King of kings. We are called to a life of surrender and obedience to the ways of God in the places where the Word and Spirit are at work in us.

The second required activity that made a lamb holy and acceptable was the removal of each leg. Our legs set the pace and direction of our journey through life. Scripture declares, *"Your word is a lamp to my feet and a light to my path"* (Ps. 119:105). To be a living sacrifice that is holy and acceptable, opening the way for transformation, our daily walk with God needs to be motivated and inspired by the Word of God. Again, Deuteronomy 8:3 is the focus here:

> *He humbled you and let you be hungry, and fed you with manna which you did not know, nor did your fathers know, that He might make you understand that man does not live*

by bread alone, but man lives by everything that proceeds out of the mouth of the Lord.

If our focus shifts to ever-increasing opinions of social media, our ethnic cultures, or prevailing philosophies, we will walk according to the course of this world (see Eph. 2:1).

The third required activity that made a lamb holy and acceptable was to be opened up so that all of the internal organs could be removed. The internal organs predominantly work together to process the food that enters the body when we eat. Jesus said of Himself that:

> *But He said to them, "I have food to eat that you do not know about." So the disciples were saying to one another, "No one brought Him anything to eat, did he?" Jesus said to them, "My food is to do the will of Him who sent Me and to accomplish His work"* (John 4:32-34).

To be a living and holy sacrifice, we must both eat the food offered us by the Father and process it internally—not through our personal turmoil but rather through His peace, love, and joy. Our ways of processing need to be exchanged for His ways of processing the events in our lives.

The soil of our hearts is well prepared as we pay attention to these three areas of our inner world. We are transformed into His likeness as we bring them into alignment through becoming a living and holy sacrifice acceptable to the Lord.

> *And the one on whom seed was sown on the good soil, this is the man who hears the word and understands it; who indeed bears fruit and brings forth, some a hundredfold, some sixty, and some thirty* (Matthew 13:23).

My third recommendation for you to experience a lifestyle of spiritual formation is that you prioritize a purposeful and focused approach that is established in the context of community. (My first recommendation was some suggested reading and my second was a suggested framework.)

The way we learn is not through a "one size fits all" methodology. We uniquely combine auditory, visual, and kinesthetic modalities in the way we learn. Consequently, when we are looking for a purposeful and focused approach to pursuing our spiritual formation, we need a vehicle that accommodates the various learning processes.

What we learn grows, develops, and matures through application and practice. The most celebrated musicians in the world practice the basics regularly. The same applies to sports and so many other endeavors in life. The idiom "practice makes perfect" remains as true today as it was when it was first coined. When we are looking for a purposeful and focused approach to pursuing our spiritual formation, we need a vehicle that enables us to practice and activate what we are learning.

For many of us, discipline is elusive. The vast majority of people need to be regularly encouraged to continue with what they are practicing. One of the most effective ways to facilitate this is to connect with a coach who is available for purposeful and focused sessions. In our busy worlds, digital access to such input from trusted and proven coaches is readily available online or electronically and is an invaluable resource.

We engage trainers, educators, and experts to assist us in many fields of endeavor in our work and personal lives. We invest in the services of builders, gym instructors, art teachers, and mechanics who provide experience, skills, ideas, knowledge, and understanding. Investing in the services of a spiritual coach is equally worth a commitment that acknowledges the priority we place on pursuing our spiritual formation to enhance our growth.

Utilizing a coach in our learning and practice is available in every area of life. Whether it be children playing sports or developing their creativity, an adult training and being educated for a new career, or the development of life skills for parenting or marriage, it requires a financial investment. Our financial decisions always reveal our priorities. When we are looking for a purposeful and focused approach to pursuing our spiritual formation, as evidence that it is a priority we will make a financial investment.

The Bible is clear that we all only know in part and see in part. The Jewish culture has always viewed learning as an activity that flourishes in the context of discovery through hearing and exploring a wide range of perspectives. How many times when listening to someone else have we said, "I have never thought of that!" Consequently, when we are looking for a purposeful approach to spiritual formation, we will enhance our growth by having others who have joined themselves to the same experience.

With all of this in mind, I want to commend the material from Graham Cooke found on his website, Brilliant TV (www.brillianttv.com). Here you will find Graham's remarkable teaching on a wide range of topics. In particular, the series *The Way God Walks with Us* will empower your spiritual formation journey. It pays attention to learning modalities and weekly input from a spiritual father and coach. It is accompanied by notes and activations, with a comments thread from the community who are learning together as they receive the same high-quality weekly input.

When you go to www.brillianttv.com you can sign up for a free seven-day trial to explore the extraordinary content and application Graham offers. Following are the notes and activities from three episodes to help you imagine what you will be invited to discover and activate.

Notes

1. Sparknotes, "Les Misérables Plot Overview," accessed September 27, 2020, https://www.sparknotes.com/lit/lesmis/summary.
2. Ibid.

> Season 1, Episode 5

THE POWER STRANDS OF PROCESS

"God sets the pace. He won't do it all at once. He'll just focus on one attribute of who He wants to be for you now, and then walk with you through your thinking, your emotions, and your perceptions... He's happy to walk with you one Truth at a time and to do it well so that you experience all the freedom of the Truth for the rest of your life."

—Graham Cooke

As we experience and learn God's ways of seeing, thinking, and feeling, our own are transformed until our language and actions reflect more and more of His true nature.

Key Truths

- God focuses on our transformation in three Power Strands of Process:
  - Vision—how we perceive God, ourselves, and our world
  - Thinking—our mind-sets and patterns of thought
  - Emotions—our feelings and emotional responses

- We behold the ways of God and He breaks through our old vision, thinking, and emotions with the beauty of His.
- God focuses on one area of transformation at a time.
- For every negative perception, mind-set, and emotion, God has the gift of one of His instead.

Key Scriptures

- Isaiah 55:9
- John 5:19
- Mark 12:30
- 1 Peter 5:7

Activation 1: One at a Time

That Truth is central to enjoying how God walks with us in our process of growth and development. We have seen too many people become overwhelmed and give up because they tried to tackle everything at once.

The areas that you've realized need an upgrade have been there for a long time. God knows that and has loved and accepted you unchangingly. You're the only one surprised. He's not!

God is celebrating that you're seeing more of the life He's always seen with you. He's delighted to focus on just one area at a time. So:

- Ask Him what area of your life He wants to focus on now.
- When you know, write it down.

- What negative expectations or speculations are you becoming aware of?
- What would new speculations of God's goodness sound like instead?
- Or, who are you going to become and what are you going to learn?
- What are the lenses that you're perceiving Him, yourself, and your circumstances with?

If Jesus were looking through your eyes, how would He see this?

- What patterns of thinking have not been helpful?
- Ask the Holy Spirit how He would think about this and rejoice in Him as your Helper.
- Describe your emotional pattern of response to this area. For any negatives, what are the emotions of God that He wants to share with you?

You can do some initial journaling in your notebook on these, but most likely you will get greater clarity over time—so continue to revisit these questions.

What you're learning most is that God delights in these conversations. He simply celebrates your growing freedom.

He knows that as you learn this process of relational transformation in one area, it will happen more quickly in the next one you explore together.

Activation 2: Identifying Your Initial Response

Take note of the way in which you respond *first* to a new revelation. These are a few descriptions to get you started, but you will find more that are unique to you.

Characteristics of processing Truth first with your mind and thoughts:

- You love to love God with your mind and think deeply with Him.
- You have a heart that treasures and values wisdom.
- You are energized by the idea that God's thoughts are higher than your thoughts.
- You enjoy ideas and truths that unfold over time.

Characteristics of processing Truth first with your heart and emotions:

- You remember most how you *felt* when you heard a new revelation.
- You may easily feel the pain of others and be moved with compassion.
- You're passionate about what you're seeing and experiencing, often sharing with friends.
- When you know and experience that God and others care, you feel cared for.

Characteristics of processing Truth first through vision/ perception:

- You're observant, taking note of things that others often miss.

- You can often see both sides of an issue or more than one possibility.
- You feel God's perspective is important and you have a passion to see things the way He does.

Again, this is not a prescriptive list. It's a *descriptive catalyst* to your conversation with the Lord about how He created you. We all have an initial starting point to our process, but it is vital to explore and establish all three.

Language and Actions

In recognizing and exploring these Power Strands of Process, you will see transformation in your *language* and *actions* as evidence of your development in the future.

Take note of any negativity or poor expectations that are present when you speak now—and notice when your language begins to better reflect your new vision, thinking, and emotions: "I used to say this…but now I find myself saying…"

Do the same thing with your responses and actions: "I used to respond negatively like this…and now it is becoming natural to respond like…" and "I used to act like this…and now I'm more likely to…"

These are your evidences of transformation!

Remember, it is all a process and these are activations that you can engage in over the coming weeks and months. Be kind to yourself as you're learning.

Season 1, Episode 6

PROCESS IS DEVELOPED IN IDENTITY

> "What you learn in your process, you get to live in your identity."
>
> —Graham Cooke

This episode offers a map as you further explore the process of becoming more like the true nature of God that you're experiencing, encountering, and beholding

Identity is where we become what we've been beholding in God. It's a process. One Truth, one area of our identity at a time as we are growing up into all things in Christ.

In process, God develops His relationship with you. In your identity, you establish your fellowship with Him.

Each process has three areas of transformation:

- Learning the gift of presence that God has created for you in your particular life situation
- The act of becoming, of practicing the gift of presence
- Then establishing the breakthrough as a lifestyle as it becomes our identity—who we really, really are in Christ

Key Scriptures

- 2 Corinthians 3:18
- Ephesians 4:20-24

Activation

1. What do you want to put off?

- Identify an old negative vision, thinking, or feeling that has not been helpful.
- Once you identify one of these, what are the other two negative perceptions that partner with it?

Example: If the Holy Spirit illuminates an "old-man" way of thinking, what are the negative perceptions (vision) and emotions (feeling) that come with that?

2. Renew your commitment to presence.

We don't *ask* for the presence of the Lord; we rejoice in it because He promised to never leave us nor forsake us. Whether His is present to your faith or to your feelings, He is present because He promised to be.

- Spend time rejoicing and thanking God that He abides in you.
- Declare your trust in Him is ever-present and never-changing in His love.
- Express your delight that as He abides in you, you abide in Him.
- Ask Him how *He* does it. Explore Scripture and the stories of Jesus.
- Worship and give thanks until joy and quiet confidence rise up.

3. Receive the gift that God has for you instead.

Isaiah 61:1-4 shows us the nature of God to make a Divine Exchange:

- For ashes, He gives beauty.
- When we mourn a loss, He gives the healing oil of joy.
- If our spirits become heavy and sad, He clothes us in praise that is living and light, making Him greater than any adversity we face.

God's opposite of everything is a gift, and gifts need to be received. They are not earned.

As we put off and let go of the old, we are able to take hold of the gift of God, unpack it with the Holy Spirit, and anticipate putting it on and living in it!

4. Practice putting on the new.

- Learn to identify your practice opportunities and make the most of them!
- Everyday challenges are a valuable training ground. The old lens is to see them as "problems." Your new lens sees them as "practice possibilities."
- Enjoy the learning as much as God does.
- He understands it will take time. Find ways to remind yourself of His delight in walking with you as you discover the magnificence of His provision.
- Ask daily: "What did I learn?"
- Some days you learn how your new ways of thinking, feeling, and seeing work. On other days, you'll forget and default to familiar old patterns. It's all part of growing and it's all valuable. Discover the learning in *every* day.

5. Consider your confession.

- Write out who you are and are becoming in this process.
- Create a description of how you will see, think, and feel once this area of development has become your lifestyle.
- Describe who God has been and has promised to be for you in this new way of living. How was and is He walking with you?

When the enemy schemes to discount your development, using default behavior as evidence, you can use this to respond: "That may be true, but the *Truth* is that *this* is who God is for and in me, and *this* is who I'm becoming because of that!"

Continue to love the learning!

Season 1, Episode 7

BEHOLDING AND BECOMING

In our worldly thinking, we value activity. Our self-image and worth is often dependent on how much we do and achieve.

But God's greatest desire is to walk with us. To *be* with us in a daily, intimate, living relationship—because *that* is where the true process of transformation occurs.

As we behold who He really is, we learn to become more like Him.

Key Scriptures

- 2 Corinthians 3:16-18
- 2 Corinthians 4:16
- Philippians 4:13

Activation

The prophetic word below is your place of activating your learning. In exploring the way God walks with us, His voice to your heart has a transformational impact that teaching does not.

He spoke creation into being and His voice continues to create us anew in Christ. We're saved once, but we're being redeemed every day, discovering just how great this salvation is.

- When it seems good to you and the Holy Spirit, begin to read and think deeply about this word.
- Take note of the key phrases that quicken your heart when you listen and read this word.
- Make a list of the promises in this word and choose one to focus on in your dialogue with the Lord.
- Begin to ask God questions. Every prophetic word is a catalyst to a relational conversation with God.

We anticipate Him being magnificent to you in this process.

Conclusion

Prophetic Word Excerpted from "Beholding and Becoming"

Cross over, My children—from all you have known, seen, and tasted of My presence.

For all that has passed before you on the journey of worship has been to bring you to this place.

For I am taking the heart of stone out of the lives of My people, to free them from selfish restraint and self-preoccupation—that they may behold Me.

In these days, I will be your reward as you worship. You will enter into that place of adoration that the angels occupy around My throne.

For it shall be on earth even as it is in heaven. Worship from earth shall ascend and meet worship descending from heaven.

When the first heaven meets the third heaven in adoration, all that is demonic in the second heaven shall be displaced by the weight of glory.

For I shall come down into that place of adoration—as you seat Me on the throne of your passion.

> When I come, all things will change. I will adorn My bride with My beauty and make her ready for My intimate embrace.
>
> Cross over, My children.
>
> Set your heart to cross over into a new land of worship.

As I wrote in the Preface:

> The apostle Peter recognized the significance of understanding that being radically restored to oneness with God should result in our pursuit of being radically restored to oneness with one another. In Second Peter 1:5 he writes: *"Now for this very reason also, applying...."* In verses two to four, Peter describes how we have become one with God and can now live in oneness with God by, "becoming partakers of the divine nature." It is for this reason that we are to apply ourselves to a lifestyle that ultimately results in brotherly kindness and love, that is, oneness with others.
>
> Peter then stresses the absolute centrality of building our spirituality on oneness with God and one another when he declares:
>
> *For if these qualities are yours and are increasing, they render you neither useless nor unfruitful in the true knowledge of our Lord Jesus Christ. For he who lacks these qualities is blind or short-sighted, having forgotten his purification from his former sins* (2 Peter 1:8-9).
>
> It then appears that he is not content that he has adequately explained the significance of following Jesus through a focus on oneness with God and others, and so he then goes on to write:

Therefore, brethren, be all the more diligent to make certain about His calling and choosing you; for as long as you practice these things, you will never stumble; for in this way the entrance into the eternal kingdom of our Lord and Savior Jesus Christ will be abundantly supplied to you (2 Peter 1:10-11).

Finally, he sees it as a privilege and necessity to definitely remind them of the need to live this way from oneness with God and others. Even when he has passed away, they would call this teaching to mind.

Therefore, I will always be ready to remind you of these things, even though you already know them, and have been established in the truth which is present with you. I consider it right, as long as I am in this earthly dwelling, to stir you up by way of reminder, knowing that the laying aside of my earthly dwelling is imminent, as also our Lord Jesus Christ has made clear to me. And I will also be diligent that at any time after my departure you will be able to call these things to mind (2 Peter 1:12-15).

Summary

Grace is the empowering presence of God. It is the strength God gives us to live from the inheritance of being in Christ and be like Jesus in every circumstance through life. Grace is much more than unmerited favor. Grace is opposed to being earned, yet it celebrates effort.

How we experience God can lead us away from relying on His great grace and living from what we have received. For example, when:

- God is viewed as inspecting and demanding,
- God is viewed as being disappointed in us,
- God is viewed as distant.

To live in the fullness of our inheritance, we must acquire information that is applied through grace and practice, resulting in transformation that grows or is established into a lifestyle.

Relational learning is a slow learning.

We are to stay in tune with the Holy Spirit so that we are aligned to the process He has designed to help us.

We are used to "earning" our qualifications through training and education—our performance.

Jesus offers us a place of transformation where He will enable an exchange of inner turmoil for His peace.

Being transformed by the renewing of the mind requires us to present our lives to God in the same way the priests offered a sacrificial lamb.

Questions and Activity

1. How have you learned to both receive and walk in God's grace?
2. How would you describe the ways you experience God?
3. How would you describe your style of learning with God, and if it is not relational, why?
4. If you were to present yourself to God as a "sacrificial lamb" for the purpose of transformation, what do you think He would draw your attention to?
5. What would need to change for you to embrace a purposeful pursuit of learning how to walk with God?

About Peter McHugh

Peter McHugh's life has regularly been turned upside down when the Lord has sovereignly interrupted him. These encounters have resulted in profound insights into the love of God and the nature of His Kingdom. He shares these revelations in his books and lives them out. He is a sought-after speaker, mentor, leader, and pastor to pastors. He lives in Melbourne, Australia with his wife Lyn, three children, and nine grandchildren.

Experience a personal revival!

Spirit-empowered content from today's top Christian authors delivered directly to your inbox.

Join today!
lovetoreadclub.com

Inspiring Articles
Powerful Video Teaching
Resources for Revival

Get all of this and so much more, e-mailed to you twice weekly!

LOVE TO READ CLUB

by **D** DESTINY IMAGE